913.3

Everyday Life of
The Barbarians

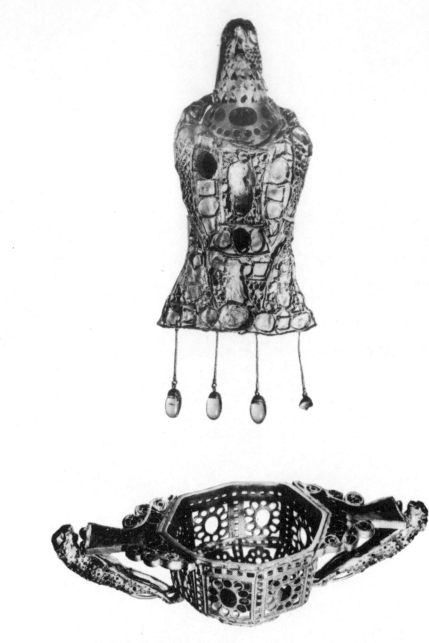

*Gold objects from the Pietroassa Treasure (Rumania)*

# Everyday Life of
# THE BARBARIANS

## Goths, Franks
## and Vandals

### MALCOLM TODD

*With drawings by Eva Wilson*

DORSET PRESS
New York

*For Kate and Richard*

Text © Malcolm Todd, 1972
Drawings © B. T. Batsford Ltd, 1972


This edition published by Dorset Press,
a division of Marboro Books Corporation,
by arrangement with
B. T. Batsford Ltd.
1988 Dorset Press


ISBN 0-88029-176-1


Printed in the United States of America

M 9 8 7 6 5 4 3 2 1

# CONTENTS

# THE ILLUSTRATIONS

# The Illustrations

# ACKNOWLEDGEMENTS

I must thank several institutions and individuals for illustrations used in this volume. Rijksdienst voor Oudheidkundige Bodemonderzoek, Amersfoort (Dr J. A. Brongers), for figs 7, 42, 71, 73 and 74; Fries Museum, Leeuwarden (Mr G. Elzinga), figs 4, 43, 44 and 59; the Danish National Museum, Copenhagen (Dr E. Munksgaard), figs 2, 37, 72 and 78; Statens Historiska Museet, Stockholm (Miss B. Straubinger), figs 50, 75–77, and 79–82; Prof. M. Stenberger, fig. 17; Historisk-archaeologisk forsøgscenter, Lejre, Denmark, fig. 26; Rheinisches Landesmuseum, Bonn (Dr. W. Janssen), fig. 48 and the jacket illustration; Schleswig-Holsteinisches Landesmuseum, Schleswig, figs 5 and 38; the Archaeological Institute, Bucharest (Prof. D. M. Pippidi), figs 63–4. My particular thanks are due to Mrs Eva Wilson, who has prepared the greater part of the line-drawings. Many others have assisted in various ways. The greatest of my debts is to my Nottingham colleague Prof. D. A. Bullough, who in discussion has never failed to stimulate thought about the oldest of controversies or the newest of discoveries. Several sections of the book owe much to his criticism at an early stage.

M.T.

# Introduction

The writer who attempts to describe the way of life of the early Germans is bound at the outset to make it clear who his Germans are. Mine are the peoples who inhabited north-western Europe beyond the frontiers of the Roman Empire, and who later transformed the western provinces of that Empire by settling widely in them. I have tried to avoid an excess of dates in this book, but the span of time which it covers extends from the second century BC, when the German peoples first came to the serious notice of the civilised nations of the Mediterranean world, to the time of the great folk-movements in the fourth, fifth and sixth centuries AD. In geographical terms the canvas is very broad. The area where we first encounter the Germans is the north German plain with the great valleys of the Elbe and the Weser, the peninsula of Denmark, and southern Norway and Sweden. By the sixth century, the descendants of those peoples had penetrated into virtually every corner of Europe and some adventurous spirits had passed beyond its borders.

Outside modern Germany and Scandinavia, not many people are familiar with the culture of the Germanic peoples before their great migratory movements. The Franks, Alamanni and Goths, if they are known at all, are as remote as the Masai or the Maya. This is unfortunate but not altogether surprising. Like the Celts and the Slavs, the Germans have never been lost and dramatically rediscovered, as were the Sumerians or the Hittites. From the Renaissance at least, the German has been a familiar figure. Usually, however, only one aspect of his affairs was comprehended. Normally, he appeared on the margins of the Roman world as a warrior, an opponent of Rome. This view of the early Germans persisted until well on into the nineteenth century and it is taking a long time to die out. Even to modern Germans down to the beginning of the twentieth century, their barbarian ancestors seemed to lie well outside the main stream of world history. The Victorians saw the Ancient Britons (now also a dying race) in much the same way. Like the Ancient Britons, the early Germans have had to wait for the archaeologists of the twentieth century to discover their true place in human history.

Every book has its bias. The bias of this one is twofold. First, it has been written from a standpoint within the Roman Empire. This is, I believe, inevitable since the written sources for the early Germans are almost wholly Greek and Roman. Secondly, I have used the archaeological evidence much more freely than that of literature. Archaeology is now recognised as a vital source of information, not only for the culture of the Germanic peoples, but also for their early history. But archaeological evidence, even for daily life, has severe limitations. At first sight it may seem to offer a great deal, but in truth there are many aspects which archaeology can never reveal. The archaeology of a pre-literate people tells us most about their settlements, homes, household utensils, their means of subsistence, way of making war, their burial-rites and, to a limited extent, their ideas of the supernatural. These are the aspects on which I have concentrated.

In suggesting books and papers for further reading, I have selected primarily works in English, though one or two classic works in German and French could not be omitted. The reader will bear in mind that this selection is decidedly arbitrary, since only a tiny fraction of the literature on the early Germans is in English. The English works which I have listed, however, are reliable and useful, and some, such as H. M. Chadwick's *The Origin of the English Nation*, are by any standard classics.

# The world
# of the Germans

## THE EMERGENCE OF THE GERMANS

The first accounts of the barbarian peoples in the extreme north of Europe were reaching the Mediterranean world in the late sixth and fifth centuries BC. The earliest Greek writers known to have had some knowledge of northern Europe, Hekateus in the sixth century and Herodotus in the fifth, made no mention of Germans. For these writers the northern barbarians were divided into Celts in the north-west and Skyths, or Scythians, in the north-east. Isolated notices of people who were much later recognised as Germans begin in the fourth century BC. In the first half of this century, Pytheas, a Greek merchant from *Massilia* (Marseilles in southern France), made a famous journey in north-western waters, in the course of which he circumnavigated Britain. Pytheas also learned something of the coastal areas of northern Germany, for he mentions the Teutones, a German people settled in Denmark, who, three hundred years later, were to burst in upon the Roman world and bring about the first great confrontation between the Roman legions and German warriors. It is clear that several later writers borrowed from Pytheas' account and it is probable that he had recorded a good deal about continental Germany —all of it unhappily now lost.

The great invasion of southern Europe by peoples calling themselves Cimbri and Teutones at the end of the second century BC first made the Romans aware of the power of the northern peoples and the threat they posed to Rome's northern frontier. Unfortunately, although a fair account of this short-lived but violent invasion can be reconstructed, we have no contemporary observations of the culture and character of the invaders themselves. But even the outline of the story itself is gripping. The Cimbri and Teutones began a joint migration *en masse* southward from their northern homeland. This was no mere warrior-raid, for they had their womenfolk and children with them in their waggons. The movement had probably been forced upon them by an extensive encroachment on their land by the sea, perhaps culminating in a great inundation like that of October 1634, which drastically altered the coastline of Friesland and its islands.

At first their trek led them into Bohemia and thence into what is now Jugoslavia. They then turned westward and, as they were now nearing the northern borders of Italy, a Roman army was sent to intercept them. That army crashed to defeat at Noreia near the modern town of Ljubljana and the Germans continued westward. Ignoring Italy, they reached eastern France by 110 BC and hoped to settle near the Roman frontier enclosing Provence. The two sides again came to blows and again the legionaries were humbled. After more travels north up the Rhône valley they smashed another Roman army at Orange. It was to take one of Rome's greatest generals and a major reform of the army to defeat the invaders. The rambling route, together with the fact that whole families were involved, must mean that they were seeking new land on which to settle. Indeed, on at least one occasion they asked the Romans for territory but the request was refused. They did not from the outset, then, seek to pitch themselves into the Roman provinces.

This dramatic meeting of north and south sharpened the interest of Graeco-Roman writers in the northern barbarians. The Greek writer Poseidonius, active in the first half of the first century BC, produced an account, now lost, of the invasion of Cimbri and Teutones which was much used in later compilations. He was the first to distinguish the Germans from the Celts and Scythians as a separate barbarian people. During his later years there occurred the second great confrontation of Rome with the Germans—Julius Caesar's campaigns in eastern France against a horde of would-be migrant Germans, led by Ariovistus. Caesar not only described these campaigns himself. He also gave a description of German social organisation and customs which, although it may have relied to some extent upon the accounts of men like Poseidonius, was informed by personal experience of the peoples settled along both banks of the middle Rhine. But it must be remembered that Caesar was not primarily a dispassionate ethnographer. He was an aspirant for the highest political offices and to the historian such men are dangerous. Naturally, Caesar built up his own achievements as best he could in his *Commentaries* and he did it by presenting the Germans as a savage and implacable foe of the Roman state. By emphasizing the savagery and power of the German warriors, he underlined his own services to the state in baulking their encroachment upon Gaul.

Caesar was the first, though not the last, Roman writer to describe the Germans as utter savages—*feri*. The Gauls could be civilised by contact with Rome: the Germans remained *feri*. This distinction between Gauls and Germans is particularly stressed by Caesar. He made the Rhine a great dividing-line between Gaul and German, although admitting that in earlier times some tribes had crossed the river from Germany and settled in northern Gaul. This insistence upon the Rhine as a clear boundary between the Celtic and the German peoples is now recognised to be an invention of Caesar's propaganda. The peoples living to the east of the middle Rhine in particular were neither purely Celtic nor Germanic, but were more indebted to the Celts in their material culture than to the Germans. This point we must return to.

After Caesar, the Rhine (now Rome's northern frontier in western Europe) was not crossed by a Roman army with imperial aims for some forty years. Then, from about 12 BC to AD 9, a series of campaigns was mounted by the emperor Augustus with the intention of finding a frontier north-east of the Rhine valley, probably along the Elbe. This great contest was won by the barbarians. The Roman armies were pulled back to the west bank of the Rhine and major expansion of Roman power beyond the Rhine and Danube was abandoned. As a result of this renewed contact with the dwellers east of the Rhine, new knowledge about Germany began to flow in. Trade-contacts began to make the barbarians of the north much less remote, and writers of the first century AD, especially the Elder Pliny, steadily increased Roman familiarity with them. Almost at the end of the century, in AD 98, there appeared

one of the first works of the historian Tacitus, a short treatise on the land of Germania and its inhabitants. The *Germania*, as it is generally known, was something of a tract for its time, but it was also a most detailed account of German institutions and customs and is the only such monograph devoted to a barbarian people to reach us from antiquity. Renaissance scholars called it a Golden Book, and so it is. Tacitus had no personal experience of the peoples he describes, but the observations of Roman officers and merchants would provide him with information which was independent of Poseidonius and Caesar and, of course, up to date. This is our main source for the early Germans.

After the brilliant light thrown by the *Germania*, there follows a virtual Dark Age. Not until the fourth century do the surviving literary works have anything worthwhile to say about the Germans. Since major movements and regroupings of peoples occurred in the intervening period, this is an irreparable loss. During the second century an artificial frontier was established by the Romans to link the middle Rhine valley with the Danube near Regensburg. This frontier, known as the Upper German and Raetian *limes* after the Roman provinces of *Germania Superior* and *Raetia* which it bounded, endured only until about 260. Then it crumpled under barbarian pressure— the first Roman frontier to collapse in western Europe.

ARCHAEOLOGY AND THE GERMAN PEOPLES

An abundant and steadily growing source of information about the early Germans is that provided by archaeology. For many regions of barbarian Europe, it is the only source. A century ago, the contribution of archaeology would have been described in terms of the striking finds from richly furnished graves and from votive deposits in peat-bogs. Now the subject is served by a whole battery of field and laboratory techniques which can be brought into play in studying most of the activities of early man.

First, what light has archaeology thrown on the origins of the Germans? This subject has a notorious past, particularly in the Third Reich. Now, however, it is possible to study the problem in a calmer atmosphere. The emergence of a more or less stable agricultural economy occurred in southern Scandinavia and northern Germany about the beginning of the third millenium BC, Neolithic culture now replacing the Mesolithic hunters and food gatherers. Precisely what gave rise to this major change in the economics of subsistence is disputed. Probably agriculture was brought to the north by new settlers from the south and south-east. Later, in the late Neolithic and early Bronze Age, there were other intrusions into the same regions, producing a distinctive Bronze Age culture based on mixed farming. Thereafter down to the Roman period, there is no sign of any major interruption in the cultural tradition. Settlement-types, forms of burial and pottery styles continued without any notable external influences, as though the population of this embryonic Germania remained largely undisturbed. A similar picture is given by examination of the skeletal material from cemeteries of this long period.

All this is in accord with what Tacitus has to say about German origins: 'I am inclined to believe that the Germans are indigenous and very little affected by immigration and by intercourse with other peoples.' And again: 'I accept the view of those who believe that the German peoples have never been tainted by intermarriage with other nations, but stand out as an individual, pure and indeed unique nation.' After the amalgam of different elements which appears to have occurred during the Neolithic, this indeed seems to have been the case.

Archaeological evidence for the various divisions of the Germans is an even more contentious subject. Archaeologists expend a great deal of time and ink in distinguishing what they call 'cultures', that is assemblages of similar metalwork and pottery types, settlement forms, house types and other cultural traits. These are normally shown to have occupied a distinct area of settlement and in the past it has often been tempting to identify these 'culture-provinces' with particular peoples or tribes. With regard to the early Germans, this linking of archaeological cultures with the tribal groups mentioned by Roman writers was carried to the ultimate limits in the early decades of the twentieth century by a leading German scholar, Gustav Kossinna and his disciples. Kossinna's views have never been accepted without serious question but they have nonetheless proved very difficult to eradicate entirely. It is indeed impossible to demonstrate identity between a culture-province and an individual population-group in the northern Iron Age, and archaeologists now prefer to leave on one side questions concerning the ethnic significance of archaeological material. When he defines cultures, the archaeologist does so primarily to provide a convenient framework for his data.

The archaeology of the early Germans has produced a literature of immense proportions and it would be foolhardy to summarize its main outline in one volume, much less a few paragraphs. It will be enough to comment on the principal areas of Germanic settlement. The main settlement-groups defined by archaeology are four: a North Sea group in southern Scandinavia and on the northern continental coast, a Western group between the Rhine and the Saale and from the Weser to the Main, an Elbe group covering the Elbe basin and extending eastward to the Oder, and finally an Eastern group between the Oder and the Vistula. What these groups represent is difficult to say, but they were not tribal confederacies. More probably they were groups of peoples sharing a common trade in material things. It is very hazardous to identify the tribes mentioned by Tacitus and the other writers within these groupings, but the following classification will not be far wrong. The North Sea group included the Chauci, the Frisii and the several smaller tribes north of the Elbe among whom the writer Ptolemy numbers the Saxons. The Western group embraced several peoples familiar to the Roman frontier administrators: the Chatti, Cherusci, Bructeri and Tencteri. The Elbe-Germans comprised the Semnones, Langobardi (Lombards), Hermunduri and the Marcomanni before they moved into Bohemia. The Eastern group are shadowy figures in the literary sources: Burgundians, Rugii, Vandals and the Goths.

Apart from informing us about the cultural and trade relations between the various regions of Germania, archaeology has performed the inestimable service of illumining the material conditions of its people. As we will see when dealing with settlement sites, the excavations of the past fifty years have provided a sound basis from which to question the statements of ancient writers and even to formulate alternative views. An enormous amount has been learnt about the various kinds of settlements, house-types and domestic equipment, technical achievement and, above all, about economic conditions. Ancillary work by biologists has added valuable knowledge of the domestic animals kept and the palaeo-botanist has enabled reconstruction of the contemporary environment through the study of plant- and pollen-remains. Yearly by these means our picture of the conditions of life is being improved and sharpened.

## GERMANS AND CELTS

Archaeology makes it clear, as no ancient writer does, that there were close contacts between the German peoples and the Celts. These are manifest not so much in the field of trade as in broad cultural affinities between central and northern Europe. These are expressed in the humble metalwork of everyday life, the brooches, pins and shears, and in the pottery. They establish very clearly that there was no abrupt dividing line between Celt and German in the centuries about the time of the birth of Christ. Writers like Caesar and Tacitus have greatly obscured the truth of this by insisting on the Rhine as a cultural frontier between Celts to the west and Germans to the east. That this distinction is false is demonstrated not only by the archaeological evidence but also by the evidence of personal- and place-names. The peoples living to the east of the Rhine and between the valleys of the Main in the south and Weser in the north were strongly influenced by Celtic culture, though they were not themselves Celtic. Nor were they, in the time of Caesar and Tacitus, Germanic. Their origins are obscure but they may perhaps have been an old grouping of tribes which had resisted the westward advance of German culture in the late Bronze Age and early Iron Age.

Celtic influence on German material culture is especially clear in the sphere of war-gear. Shields, swords and spear-heads in the north from the first century BC onward frequently reveal a derivation from Celtic types, and many weapons which are themselves of Celtic manufacture occur in the same regions. No doubt this influence is due to warfare between Celts and Germans as well as to trade. Celtic influence is apparent in other fields as well, metalwork in particular. Several of the most remarkable products of Celtic craftsmen have been found in Germania. The most striking have come from Denmark: the two richly ornamented carts from Djebjerg (Jutland), the silver cauldron from Gundestrup (Himmerland),

and the huge bronze cauldron from Brå (Jutland). By any standards these are superb products and they are the most spectacular of German borrowings from the Celts.

## THE GERMANS AND THEIR EASTERN NEIGHBOURS

There were contacts, too, with peoples to the east. Before the birth of Christ, the Slavs had begun to move westward from eastern Poland, reaching in due course the river Dnieper, where they came into contact with the Goths and other east Germans. Until their permanent settlement in the present-day Slav territories, not a great deal is known about their material culture. From the south-east, came a branch of steppe nomads, the Sarmatians, who began to encroach upon the Pontic area about 200 BC, extending their area of settlement thence west of the Dnieper and into Rumania and Poland. By the third century AD this region must have been an extraordinary melting-pot of cultures: Greek, Dacian, Sarmatian, Slav and Goth. To the north-east of the Germans lay the Balts of East Prussia, Poland and western Russia. This region was in touch with the Roman Empire and with the Germans. As a separate grouping the Balts have been frequently overlooked. Although to a degree influenced by the east Germans, their cultural development was independent of them. About all these eastern barbarians there is precious little recorded by ancient writers, and they touch our theme at this point only. But it may be borne in mind that the east Germans lay adjacent to nomadic and semi-nomadic peoples and that they would feel the first tremors of migrations from the steppes.

It was from this direction that the most devastating of all invasions was to come. In AD 376 intelligence reached Roman officers in the garrisons on the Danube frontier that there were unusually large and widespread disturbances among the Gothic peoples to the north. All the tribes in the Black Sea region appeared to be in a ferment. Rumour had it that they had been attacked by a fearsome people from the east. Reports of barbarian movements were hardly news and the Roman garrisons at first were not moved by a fresh wave of restlessness. But then the bands of refugee Germans began to arrive on the Danube bank, becoming ever larger until a vast concourse of Goths had gathered on the borders of the Empire. The savage people who had fallen on them were the Huns. They were to terrorize much of Europe for less than a century, but in that relatively short time they earned an undying reputation for barbarous cruelty. The Huns were not Germanic, but since their history is so bound up with that of the Goths and other Germans, they cannot be forced out of the narrative, any more than they could be driven from the lands of the Romans and the Goths.

It was about AD 370 that the Huns came into contact with the Goths. Before this their homeland had been the steppes of south Russia, where they lived as nomads in conditions of the basest poverty and hardship. Surprisingly little is known for certain about them before they launched their attack on the Goths. Their origins are unknown. Roman writers could report little about these nomads which can be taken at all seriously. Among the Goths, not surprisingly in view of their experience of Huns, the story was current that they were the offspring of witches and evil spirits. They may have had contacts with the civilisations of the Far East. Chinese annals frequently mention a people, whom they term Hsiung-nu, and some scholars are prepared to believe that these were Huns. Like all nomadic peoples they are extremely difficult to track down by the usual techniques of archaeology. Nomads leave virtually no settlement sites behind them and often no recognizeable graves. They may use very few artifacts of metal or pottery, and even these they often acquired from other peoples. Thus what is known about them comes from Roman writers, with a little support from the archaeological record.

The Huns lived from their herds, with additional supplies of food coming from hunting and food-gathering. This economy provided them with a bare existence but no more. From childhood they were inured to hunger and thirst as necessary aspects of life. Probably some of their food supply was produced by trading with settled agricultural peoples. Their technical level is illustrated by the clothes they wore. These were of linen or animal skins sewn together, and were lived in until they fell apart piece by piece.

Like all steppe nomads, the Huns were superb horsemen, indeed they appeared to Romans to live on horseback. 'They are unable to put their feet firmly on the ground: they live and sleep on their horses', says Zosimus. Their great skill in the arts of cavalry was enhanced by their mastery of the use of the bow. These accomplishments in combination were the basis of their successes against both Roman and German infantry armies. As well as the bow, swords were carried by some warriors and others were skilled in the use of a net or lasso. Despite their extreme poverty and primitive economy, the Huns posed a tremendous military threat to the peoples they encountered in the west. Even their physical appearance was an advantage. Romans found them utterly repulsive to look on and professed to be uncertain as to whether they were men or animals.

These nomads had no kings but were ruled in time of war by their leading men. How they achieved their eminent position is not known, but probably their prowess in war won them their repute. In periods of peace there was little distinction between man and man, family and family. All the men took their share in the unending task of looking after the animals and seeking fresh pasture for them.

Although the Huns had no kings, powerful war-leaders did emerge among them. By far the most famed and successful was Attila, who together with his brother Bleda came to power in AD 433. At this time the Huns were the masters of the Germanic peoples who occupied the area between the Alps and the Baltic Sea, and almost from the Rhine to the Caspian. Their armies consisted not only of Huns but also subject peoples whom they dragged in their wake, Alans, Gepids, Slavs and Goths. From a base in what is now Hungary, Attila, eclipsing and eventually setting aside his brother, threatened the Eastern Roman Empire centred on Constantinople and the Western focused on Italy. After 440 the storm broke. Attila made a shambles of the Roman frontier on the middle Danube, destroying towns and forts, and devastated northern Greece. A more ambitious scheme of conquest was set in motion in 451, when the Huns crossed the Rhine and advanced on Orleans. Near Troyes, the Huns suffered their first major reverse at the hands of a combined Roman and Visigothic army. This was to be a turning-point. All the same, in the following year Attila mounted an invasion of North Italy, capturing Aquileia and other strongholds. But he aimed still higher and intended to march on Rome. Roman reinforcements from the east, disease among his own men and, scourge of most barbarian armies, famine, prevented him. In the midst of preparations to invade Constantinople in 453, he died. After him the great empire he had established was not restored. The Huns themselves and their subjects began to fall away from the great confederacy. Much worse for the Huns, other ferocious nomads began to sweep over the steppes after 460. Bands of Huns remained to raid their neighbours' cattle and loot their settlements, but they were a remnant only of an astonishing power.

## THE GERMANS AND ROME

Relations between Rome and the Germans are by no means an unrelieved story of conflict and destruction. The battlefield was not the only meeting-place of German and Roman. From her earliest experiments in Empire Rome realised that allied tribes beyond her frontiers were a better safeguard for the security of the provinces than a military presence on the frontiers themselves alone. Strong military garrisons were always required on the front which faced the Germans but, as on other frontiers, some reliance was also placed upon the peaceful cooperation of tribes who entered into treaty relations with the Roman state. For instance, after early contests with Rome the Frisii of northern Holland eventually settled down to a long period of untroubled co-existence with the Imperial government, gaining thereby in material advancement. A branch of the Suebi, the Suebi Nicretes, was settled with Roman approval on the fertile land of the Neckar valley, thus forming for a time an effective buffer against less amenable barbarians to the east.

In later centuries Germans played an even more immediate role in frontier defence, as soldiers in regular regiments of the Roman army. Barbarian groups were also employed as federates (*foederati*), receiving land in return for military service in the area in which they were settled. A share in the fertility of the land would, the Romans hoped, induce them to protect it against the outer ring of barbarians. These federate groups often proved effective, particularly when they consisted of a band gathered round an energetic warrior. Entire peoples or tribes under their tribal leaders proved less successful in frontier defence. In the regular army barbarians were by no means confined to the ranks. On the contrary, many of the highest ranking officers and army commanders of the late Empire were of German extraction.

In the early Empire, several German leaders served in the Roman army before rising to prominence among their own people. In some cases, some of these men wrought significant changes in the political and social structure of individual peoples. As we will see in the next chapter, the most interesting of these returned émigrés is Maroboduus of the Marcomanni, but a list of the others is eloquent testimony to how much Germans could learn in the service of Rome: Arminius, conqueror of the luckless and miscast Quinctilius Varus, Gannascus, a successful raider of the Gaulish coast in the first century AD, Cruptorix, who led a revolt among the Frisii, and finally Julius Civilis, the moving spirit of the great revolt of the Batavi in AD 69–70.

In the fields of trade and commerce also the German and Roman worlds got to know each other well. Already by the time of Caesar's invasion of Gaul, Roman traders had been attracted across the Rhine by commercial prospects. The Suebi, a confederacy of tribes occupying the Elbe basin, let the traders in to sell off surplus war-booty rather than to acquire southern luxuries. Indeed in the time of Caesar they positively forbade the import of wine into their territory, considering it was likely to sap their stamina and endurance. But not all Germans took this austere line. Roman luxuries, including wine, were beginning to find their way into wealthy barbarian households already in the first century BC. Now, as later, fine vessels of silver, and occasionally of gold, found their way across the frontiers and, ultimately, into chieftains' graves.

The grave of such a chieftain found at Hoby on the Danish island of Laaland is the earliest and the outstanding example. In this grave there lay the skeleton of a middle-aged man, together with joints of pork—the chieftain's portion in the barbarian world—and a superb table service of imported metal vessels. The finest of these were a pair of silver cups decorated in relief with scenes from Greek myth, a large bronze tray on which they had stood and several handsome bronze vessels. Other, somewhat later, finds of excellent metalwork from the Graeco-Roman world have turned up in northern Europe, but none is so splendid as that from Hoby.

2 The Hoby (Laaland) grave. A chieftain's burial of about the birth of Christ

Humbler items too crossed the frontiers in the packs of traders, some in great quantity: glassware, pottery, leather goods, coins, brooches and other ornaments. Sometimes these humdrum objects had an influence far beyond their intended sphere, in forming barbarian art-styles, much as imported Greek bronzework had given inspiration to Celtic craftsmen in the fifth century BC.

Naturally, not all these objects came into German hands as a result of long-distance trade. The great hoard of silver tableware found at Hildesheim is best interpreted as loot, gathered together over a long period before being buried in the second century AD. An even clearer case of a looted object is a bronze bucket from a burial mound at Björska in the Swedish province of Vastmanland. It had been put to service as a container for the cremated remains of a local chief, but its original function is made clear by a Latin inscription 'dedicated to Apollo Grannus by Ammillius Constans, warden of his temple'. The history of this bucket had obviously been eventful and its departure from some Roman temple hurried.

There was yet another channel besides trade and looting through which contact was maintained between north and south: diplomacy. It was customary for barbarian rulers whose cooperation was believed to be worth purchase to receive silver or gold vessels as gifts or bribes. In some cases, financial assistance of a more practical kind was proferred, in the form of coined money. Probably these subventions and gifts travelling in the 'diplomatic bag' were a customary feature of the relations between Rome and many German leaders, especially those near to the frontiers whose goodwill was more than usually worth cultivating. But we have just seen that the long arm of Rome's external contacts reached Scandinavia too. The practice continued down to the end of the Roman Empire in the west and thus presumably it achieved some results. A fine fourth-century hoard of silver plate found at Kaiseraugst near Basle is probably a relic of the same traffic, as are the numerous finds of Roman gold coins in territories occupied by the Goths at the end of the Roman period. There were exchanges in the other direction too. The Cimbri gave the emperor Augustus their most treasured cauldron, we are told by Strabo, as a sign of their friendship.

What did Germany offer in turn to Roman merchants? The main exports to the Roman Empire were slaves, furs and animal skins, and amber from the coastlands of East Prussia and Denmark. The latter commodity had been still more sought after for ornaments in the prehistoric periods, and to acquire it merchants had long before developed a trade-route leading to the amber coast from the Danube valley near Vienna, passing through Bohemia and the central German plain. Along the amber routes goods continued to travel during the Roman period. Other arteries of trade followed the valleys leading eastward from the Rhine, particularly those of the Lippe, Ruhr and Main, and thence into the valleys of the northward flowing streams of Weser and Elbe. The sea-routes round the coasts of Holland, north Germany and Denmark were also in use, and as time went on German merchant-sailors began to develop their navigational skills in these waters.

Thus it was that well before the barbarians entered the Roman provinces as conquerors, they had had a long experience of the material wealth of the Roman world. The German migrations might be pictured as savage, destructive expeditions. This is far too simplistic. They were not the result of organised schemes of conquest, nor were many of them any more destructive than the passage of any ancient army. As a recent writer has expressed it, the invasions were 'a gold-rush of immigrants from the underdeveloped countries of the north into the rich lands of the Mediterranean'. Long contact through trade and diplomacy had shown the Germans what awaited them in the south. The time had come to take it.

NEW CONFEDERACIES AND THE MIGRATIONS

During the third century AD there occurred major regroupings of the German peoples. Several of the confederacies which were now created migrated far from the territories in which they were formed, mostly into the western Roman provinces. The Alamanni ('all people') emerged as a force to be reckoned with shortly after AD 200, occupying the land between the Main and the Roman frontier. Sixty years later they battered that frontier down and settled in the fertile lands between the Rhine and the Danube. There they stayed during the fourth century and then in the early fifth pushed westwards into Gaul and south into the

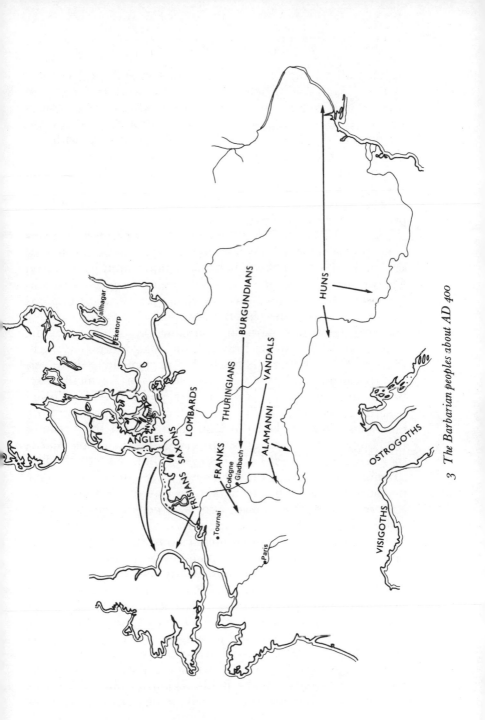

3 *The Barbarian peoples about AD 400*

Alpine valleys. Before the lower Rhine in the third century another league of peoples, the Franks, welded themselves together and pressed hard upon this front. On several occasions they burst into Gaul and in the fourth century some of them established themselves to the west of the Rhine, with the grudging support of Roman commanders.

Along the long Danube frontier, the Empire had to contend with somewhat less menacing foes, until the late fourth century at least. Shortly after AD 270, the Romans evacuated their province of Dacia (the modern Rumania) and the territory was seized by the Goths. They had possibly originated in Scandinavia, but travelled an immense distance to the south-east, settling in the Black Sea hinterland before the third century. There they separated into two major groups, Visigoths (between the Danube and the Dniester) and Ostrogoths (north-east of the Dniester). Both peoples were to range widely and play important parts in reshaping the old Empire, the Ostrogoths by occupying Italy and the Visigoths by settling in southern Gaul and later in Spain. Before they did so, however, they performed the two feats by which the Germanic barbarians are commonly remembered. In 378, after being allowed to settle in the Empire when under the severest pressure from the Huns, they crushed the Roman legions in the battle of Adrianople. More famous yet, in 410 under their king Alaric, they broke into central Italy, besieged Rome and took the city. To many people at the time the news of the fall of Rome to the northern invader seems to herald the end of the world, or at least the end of their world, and later generations up to the present have taken the same view. In actuality, the capture of Rome was a relatively insignificant event in the political and military fields of Romano-German relations. But its psychological impact was tremendous. Alaric and his followers are usually credited with the Sack of Rome in 410. In truth, few of the inhabitants seem to have been slaughtered and it was mainly the houses of the aristocracy that were looted and destroyed. The ancient buildings of Rome did not greatly suffer and the fact that Alaric was a Christian preserved the churches.

Another long migration was that of the Vandals, who by the first century AD had left the Baltic regions for Silesia. Some of them remained there, this branch being termed the Siling

Vandals. Another group, the Asdings, were more mobile and eventually crossed the Danube on to Roman territory where they were briefly employed as federates. In 406, the Vandals and a motley army of barbarians took advantage of a weakening of the Rhine frontier and a freezing of the Rhine itself to cross into Gaul. For about two years their bands raided widely over Gaul without let or hindrance. Then they crossed the Pyrenees into Spain. Two more years of raiding passed before the Roman government could achieve a temporary settlement. Rome then set an army of Visigoths upon them in the hope of reducing both barbarian threats. The policy was partially successful, for the Silings were almost annihilated. The Asdings, however, were pushed into southern Spain and found there a weapon which Rome had so far managed to keep out of barbarian hands—sea-power. The coastal towns of southern Spain fell into Vandal hands and with them the ships in their harbours. North Africa with its great supplies of grain lay at their mercy. In 429, under Gaiseric they crossed the Straits of Gibraltar and overran the fertile plains on the sea-board. Roman armies could hold on to defended strongholds but were powerless against the invaders in the field. The Vandals had to be recognised as federates, and later in 442 their king was acknowledged as the independent sovereign of North Africa.

There were other great enterprises, which carried off correspondingly great rewards. We had left the Ostrogoths in Hungary beneath the domination of the Huns. After the death of Attila they were prominent members of the league of peoples which overthrew the Hun empire. Their chance of seizing a place in the Mediterranean provinces came after the rise to power among them of the chieftain Theoderic, in 471. Under him, the Ostrogoths moved in force into the Balkans and thence, in 488, into Italy. The peninsula had been controlled since 476 by one Odoacer, the leader of the barbarian federate forces, but these were no match for Theoderic's army. By the middle of 490, he was in control of Italy and Odoacer was besieged in Ravenna. The town could not be stormed, but Theoderic's treacherous diplomacy found a way of luring out his opponent to his assassination. Italy thus passed under the rule of an Ostrogoth, but it was not a barbarian kingdom that he ruled. Theoderic, like Odoacer before him, was a vice-regent of the

Roman Emperor and Roman forms of administration were preserved. There was remarkably little mixing between Roman and German. Intermarriage was expressly forbidden, and the interests of Goths and Romans were looked after by separate officials. Even the Roman Senate continued to meet, and the law was still based on the ancient code.

The most northerly migrators, Frisians, Saxons, Angli and mixed bands of other coastal peoples had as their particular target the southeastern coasts of Britain. Despite a powerful Roman defensive system and a well-equipped fleet, these shores proved vulnerable and Germans were being settled in eastern Britain in the early fifth century. The great influx of Germanic settlers was not to start, however, until after 450.

Thus by the end of the fifth century, all of what had been the western provinces of the Empire were dominated by Germanic war-lords and their followers. Almost all of these barbarian powers, however, were to prove transient. Only the Franks indeed succeeded in setting up a political power which survived the final dissolution of Roman administration and later supplanted it. Yet, though formidable enough in the third and fourth centuries, the small bands of Frankish raiders and settlers who crossed the Rhine in the final decades of the western Empire seemed to no-one the likely successors to the Romans in these lands. But so it was to prove. An untidy amalgam of insignificant warrior bands from between the Weser and the Rhine made northern Gaul their territory and laid there the foundations of the Carolingian empire.

FURTHER READING

*General Works*

Julius Caesar, *The Conquest of Gaul* (Penguin) (translation of *De Bello Gallico*)

Tacitus, *On Britain and Germany* (Penguin) (translation of *Agricola* and *Germania*)

Gregory of Tours, *The History of the Franks* (translated by O. Dalton, Oxford)

H. M. Chadwick, *The Origin of the English Nation* (Cambridge)

A. Dopsch, *The Economic and Social Foundations of European Civilisation* (New York)

E. A. Thompson, *The Early Germans* (Oxford)

R. E. M. Wheeler, *Rome Beyond the Imperial Frontiers* (Bell)

O. Klindt-Jensen, *Foreign Influences in Denmark's Early Iron Age Acta Archaeologica* (Copenhagen) 1950

R. Hachmann, G. Kossack, H. Kuhn, *Völker zwischen Germanen und Kelten* (Neumünster)

J. M. Wallace-Hadrill, *The Barbarian West AD 400-700* (Hutchinson)

H. St. L. B. Moss, *The Birth of the Middle Ages* (Oxford)

J. B. Bury, *The Invasion of Europe by the Barbarians* (London)

Sir S. Dill, *Roman Society in Gaul in the Merovingian Age* (Macmillan)

E. A. Thompson, *The Visigoths in the Time of Ulfila* (Oxford)

P. Lasko, *The Kingdom of the Franks* (Thames and Hudson)

E. Salin, *La civilisation Merovingienne*, 4 vols. (Paris)

R. Hachmann, *The Germanic Peoples* (Barrie & Jenkins)

M. Todd, *The Northern Barbarians* (Hutchinson)

# The structure
# of society

SOCIAL ORGANISATION

The early German peoples (*civitates* as Roman writers called them) were composed of loose population-groups normally termed tribes *(pagi)* and these in turn were made up by numbers of clans or kindreds. These kindreds formed the economic units which farmed the land. They were only very loose amalgams, acting in concert rarely in time of peace. Nor must it be thought that the tribes were really cohesive units. Their organisation was in fact very primitive when the Germans emerge into history in the pages of Caesar and Tacitus. The elders of each tribe formed a council which dealt with the vital matter of the allotment of land and with major disputes. Probably it had no other function in the peacetime activities of the tribe, though it may have been responsible for some degree of organisation in war. There is not much evidence that tribe often associated with tribe to some common end, except of course in war.

Cutting across these 'natural' institutions of the tribe and the kindred, shared by very many primitive peoples all over the world, there was the institution of the retinue. This had its origin in a band of warriors gathering about a leader for a specific purpose, usually a raid for plunder. After the enterprise had been carried out, the band dispersed to enjoy their gains and later to join another raiding party. As time went on these bands became more permanent and the retinue began to approximate to a formal institution. By the end of the first century AD, the relationship between a leader and his followers (his *comites* or *comitatus*) had crystallised into something more enduring. The following was now maintained by the leader, not only during military actions of his own devising but also in peacetime. The warriors in a *comitatus* received from their leader food, sustenance, weapons and equipment.

When the leader took his retinue to war, its members fought as a discrete unit, separate from the kindreds and from other retinues of the same people, owing allegiance to their own leader and not to the elected chief of the entire *civitas*. Thus in wartime the growth of the retinues tended to disrupt the social order, for a single kindred could provide warriors for several different retinues and thus lose its most energetic sons. The retinues were also disruptive in time of peace, in that, if they were successful in their plunder raids they greatly increased the wealth, and thus the prestige, of their members over that of the rest of the kindred. Naturally, the more successful the retinue became, the more likely it was to draw on the leading warriors and their sons, thus becoming a distinct and élitist element in society. These were the men whose circumstances allowed them to be full-time warriors. The poor warrior who could not leave his household and land for long periods had little hope of entering a retinue.

Thus the companions who made up a retinue were well on the way to becoming a separate class, a warrior aristocracy whose position was guaranteed by their martial prowess. They were, however, by no means omnipotent. There are several recorded cases of a retinue and its leader incurring the hostility of the other warriors in a people and having to endure exile as a result. One of the most far-reaching and significant features of the retinues was their power to attract to the service of one man warriors from several peoples, so that some of the smaller peoples stood to lose their best warriors unless they could throw up charismatic leaders of their own. This far-ranging character of certain retinues was undoubtedly influential in binding the belligerent spirits of several peoples together. This was the first opening of the way towards the major re-groupings of German peoples in the third century AD, which were to have such profound effects on the later history of Europe.

## THE LEADERS

How were the Germanic peoples governed? On turning to the

institutions of government we come up against major difficulties. Julius Caesar says little about this and the information he does provide is difficult to integrate with later sources. Probably this is because changes occurred in the social order between the first century BC and about AD 100, particularly among those peoples now in close contact with the Roman frontiers along the Rhine and Danube. After the *Germania* of Tacitus, virtually no information is available on tribal government for more than two hundred years. Remarkably, when the Germans emerge from this Dark Age, several of their institutions of leadership have changed hardly at all.

At the time the *Germania* was written, there were three main organs in the government of Germanic peoples: the chieftainship, the council of the leading men, and the general assembly of all the warriors. As in many other tribal societies, the council of the nobles and the assembly counted for much more than the authority of most chiefs. Some chiefs were elected, normally on the strength of their valour and warlike prestige. The duties of chieftains of this kind were primarily military and often they held office only for the duration of a particular emergency or campaign. At the beginning of a war, then, the people elected a man (or occasionally two) to lead them and he supplanted any leader they may have had in peacetime.

There was also another kind of leader, whom Tacitus calls a king *(rex)*, owing his rank not to an election but to his noble, or royal, birth. The duties of this kind of chief are not clear. Sometimes he led his people in war, like the elected leaders, and indeed men of royal stock could become chieftains by election. Otherwise he possessed certain ill-defined religious or sacral functions. Choice of the successor to a king who died or was deposed was made from the entire number of those regarded as of royal stock. There was no automatic succession of father by

*4  Whalebone sceptre from Rauwerd (Friesland)*

eldest son. Although Romans called chiefs of this kind 'kings', there should be no confusion with medieval and modern ideas of what that term connotes. Their power even to influence their followers was limited and coercive powers seem hardly to have existed. A chief's power rested ultimately on his prestige or his personality. If either declined or proved inadequate, he would be deposed. He was not set apart like other men and treated as a separate individual. No divinity hedged him about as it did a medieval monarch. Even on the field of battle, though he was expected to give a lead, his orders commanded no implicit obedience.

In the Migration period the election of chieftains persisted, and the power of individual leaders was still restricted. There are many recorded cases of even the more successful German leaders consulting the council of leading warriors or the whole people and being bound by their recommendations. Thus, when the Visigoths entered the Roman Empire in 376, the decision was taken not by their king alone but by a general assembly of the people. Little is known of the internal government of the Franks, Alamanni and the rest. Among the Visigoths, however, the leader of the whole people was often referred to as the *iudex* (judge) and not as the *rex*. This name implies that these leaders had some judicial powers, although we are not told what these were. In other respects, the Migration period rulers about whom anything is known do not seem to have differed greatly from the chiefs of the time of Tacitus. Only the successful bidders for empire like Theoderic and Clovis stand out from the others, and they do so by virtue of their unparalleled achievements.

In the earlier centuries too there were exceptions. Whereas most leaders governed by influence, a few tried to assume more or less autocratic powers, with varying success. The most successful, for a time, was a king of the Marcomanni about the time of Christ, Maroboduus. He brought a new concept of government to his people, by imposing his authority on the conduct of affairs. The most significant aspect which his new style of leadership influenced was that of military organisation. Something approaching a standing army was for the first time welded together, trained and disciplined. Orders were obeyed and tactics were planned. Not for nothing had Maroboduus been educated within the Roman Empire. All this was very new to a Germanic people, and it was to remain exceptional—fortunately for the Romans. Others made the attempt to emulate Maroboduus but his brief achievement was not rivalled. Probably in most Germanic peoples social organisation was too primitive and inflexible to withstand the stresses on the constituent clans which this kind of monarchical system set up. Even Maroboduus himself was compelled to flee to the Roman Empire in AD 19 and it was to be three centuries or more before another leader was to attain such autocratic powers.

### THE PRIESTS

Like the Gauls, the Germans had a regular priestly organisation, presided over by a chief priest *(sacerdos civitatis)*. The duties of the priests involved the taking of omens on public occasions (especially on the question of going to war), acting as a kind of Speaker at meetings of the general assembly, punishing certain major offences and looking after the sacred groves and the cult-objects in them. Although they were exempted from fighting, they were also often present on the field of battle. Indeed they and not the war-leaders were responsible for carrying the sacred banners from the groves into the battle line. No doubt they also ordered the public sacrifices. With regard to their place in society, it is reasonable to compare the German priests with the Druids of the Celts, though in their legal powers they were much more limited than the Druids.

All this information is given us by Tacitus. Later sources are unfortunately meagre, but in general terms the priestly organisation of later peoples is broadly similar to that already outlined. There are, however, several interesting divergences. Among the fourth-century Burgundians, the chief priest, or *sinistus*, held his position for life and could not be ousted. One important difference is apparent in the Visigothic system of priesthood. Among this people in the fourth century, priests were attached to individual clans or tribes. In all other cases known to us they served entire peoples.

### KINSHIP AND THE FAMILY

The most cohesive bonds of early German society were those of kinship. As late as the Migration period, blood relationship

28

still commonly held together the warrior-bands within a larger grouping of tribes. Men depended for their basic security upon their kindred. Revenge and retribution for a crime or injury committed against an individual was the responsibility of his entire kin, and likewise the kin of the man who had done the injury was involved in its expiation. If the kin of the offended man were not satisfied by the terms offered by the kin of the offender, a blood-feud would be the result. The feud might sound at best a disruptive institution, leading often to chaos. More probably, total breakdown in agreement on the amount of composition was rare and the destructive forces of the feud relatively rarely unleashed.

Some judicial matters were in the hands of the leading men of each people. These 'judges' as Caesar calls them do not seem to have been invested with any formal powers. They could not compel miscreants, or even disputants, to come before them. They could only use what influence they possessed to settle the matter. Caesar knew of no formal courts at all. Any reconciliation or coercion was effected by the judges or by the parties involved in the dispute. By the time the *Germania* was compiled, the popular assembly heard suits in which the entire people had an interest. The assembly was now responsible for the election of a number of judges and these men travelled about from community to community hearing cases. Each judge took with him 100 men to back up his authority and assist him with advice.

There is very little evidence about the kinds of crimes which were prevalent in the earlier centuries, and the penalties thought appropriate for them. Hanging was the price to be paid for treason or desertion in battle. Those guilty of cowardice and those convicted of homosexual offences were thrown into swamps and forcibly drowned. A number of corpses recovered from peat bogs could well be those of wretches who had ended their lives in this appalling fashion. Branches are occasionally found holding down the limbs or lying across the body. Probably the great majority of the other offences were punished by fines levied in horses or more commonly in cattle. These were assigned partly to the injured party and partly to the people or the chief.

Both Caesar and Tacitus note the honour in which chastity

was held by the Germans and Tacitus was able to score some easy points off Roman society of his day by comparing the laxity of its standards in sexual matters with the strictness of the Germans. In the fifth century this aspect of German life could still be remarked on. Salvian called the Goths 'a treacherous people but a chaste one' and the Saxons 'ferociously cruel but remarkably chaste'. The marriage-tie, according to all the Roman observers, was strictly observed. Extra-marital affairs were a source of great shame and proven cases of adultery were severely punished. There is no mention of prostitution until the Migration period. Both young men and women tended to marry later than was the custom in Rome (i.e. than the early 'teens). How late this might be is not clear but probably the late 'teens and early twenties is meant. Warriors did not enter upon the married state until they were in the full flower of their physical strength and had proved their valour.

Probably these writers have presented too ideal a picture of the German matrimonial scene. From later German sources it is clear that in parts of medieval Germany, and no doubt in earlier times, wives were no more than chattels. They were bought like slaves and not even suffered to sit at the same table as their lords. Marriage by purchase is recorded among the Burgundians, Lombards and Saxons, and there are survivals of similar transactions in Frankish custom. Polygamy, largely ignored by Roman writers, was practised by some German leaders of the early period and by later Scandinavians and inhabitants of the Baltic coasts, generally by men of high rank only. It has ever been an expensive business. Among some peoples *suttee*, or sacrifice of the widow on the death of one of the leading men, was known. All this indicates that the honourable and even influential position of women outlined by Tacitus was by no means universal in early Germany.

That adultery was an offence which only women could commit is clear from the *Germania*. No penalty is recorded there for men, but for women adulterers there was no mercy. Her husband shaved off her hair, stripped her and drove her from the home and the village. Archaeology provides grounds for thinking that in some areas at least the death penalty was meted out for adultery. Several female corpses from northern peat-bogs have had their hair shorn, in some cases on one side

5 *Corpse of a fourteen-year-old girl from Windeby (Schleswig)*

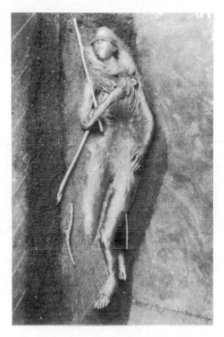

only. One striking case is a fourteen-year-old girl from Windeby in Danish Schleswig. She was found naked on her back in a hole in the peat, a hide collar round her neck and a narrow blindfold over her eyes. On the left side of her head her blonde hair had been shaven close to the skull, while on the other side it was cut to a length of about two inches. It is possible that this girl had been the victim of some religious rite rather than slain by an outraged husband, but the latter fate is not an unlikely one.

SLAVERY

The institution of slavery existed in early Germany, but it is difficult to estimate how common slaves were. In certain areas there were more slaves than in others: for instance among the Marcomanni in the second century and the Alamanni in the fourth. Both areas lay close to the Roman frontiers and their proximity had probably contributed to this development in their social structure. In the time of Caesar and Tacitus, slave labour seems not to have been common. The work which slaves might have done, the most humble domestic and agricultural tasks, were left to women and the aged. Roman prisoners of war were kept as slaves, but these unfortunates were not numerous enough to play a significant part in the economics of everyday life.

The conditions of servitude for German slaves were very different from those in the Roman Empire. Slaves had their own homes, separate from their master's. They were obliged to pay to their master at intervals quantities of grain, cloth or head of cattle. In this respect the German slave was like the Roman tenant farmer, except that he was not free. Slaves were employed on the land, but not in the large gangs which Romans were used to direct in workshops, quarries and estates. By Roman standards physical punishment by binding or beating was rare, but Tacitus suggests that the slave could be put to death with complete impunity by his master. They were probably so few because they could not be adequately maintained within the German economic order. There was little need of them, since the work of individual households could be performed by women and children. There was no large-scale industry in which slave-labour would have been useful. Though they could contribute to the economy of an agricultural community, they would be extra mouths to feed. In the undeveloped peasant economy of early Germany they would be therefore no asset.

During the Migrations the situation underwent no major change. After settlement in the western Roman provinces, however, it is plain that the number of slaves in German households increased. In addition to the sources which had earlier existed, enslavement could now be inflicted by law. Theft was the offence most commonly visited by this penalty. Nevertheless, despite this increase, the total slave population was not high. The law codes suggest that the prices of slaves were high compared with animals and other chattels. This can hardly have been so if they were in plentiful supply. Significant changes also occurred in the occupations of slaves after the Germanic settlements in the Empire. Whereas before the Migrations slaves had done domestic and agricultural tasks of the meanest kinds, in the Burgundian Laws they appear as gold and silversmiths, bronzeworkers, carpenters, cobblers and even tailors. No doubt a large proportion of these slaves with special skills were Greek and Roman craftsmen. Evidently the delights of life within the Roman Empire were being tasted to the full by the barbarians.

## FURTHER READING

The Roman literary sources for Germanic society are fully discussed by E. A. Thompson, *The Early Germans*, Chaps 1 & 2. H. M. Chadwick, *The Origin of the English Nation* is a classic which still has much to offer. On kingship, an important contribution is J. M. Wallace-Hadrill, *Early Germanic Kingship in Britain and on the Continent* (Oxford).

# 3

# Settlements
# and the land

To Roman writers, Germany was almost synonymous with forest and swamp. The common impression of the lands inhabited by the northern barbarians is succinctly expressed by Tacitus: 'In general the country, although quite varied in character, either bristles with forests or is foul with swamp.'

This picture needs considerable modification. Large areas certainly were occupied by forest throughout the period and as late as the eleventh century AD Adam of Bremen still had some basis for remarking that all of Germany was covered in forest. Deep forest continued to cover great tracts until long after Adam's time. Some of it still survives, to depress the traveller across central Germany. But in actuality there were many areas in which man had made appreciable inroads upon the surrounding forest long before the time of Tacitus, or even of Caesar. This clearance of the forest was effected by the felling and burning of selected areas of trees, a practice adopted centuries earlier by Neolithic settlers in Europe and used until comparatively recent times in parts of Sweden. As well as releasing new land from the grip of the forest, this slash-and-burn clearance (*Rodung* as it is called in Germany) meant that the land was temporarily enriched with mineral salts from the wood-ash. After one area of land had been cultivated for several years, its mineral content was drained away beneath a level needed to support a crop. It was therefore abandoned again to the wild, to be reclaimed once more after a lapse of ten or more years when the tree-cover had returned. The clearance of forest received a great boost with the coming of iron to northern Europe in the sixth century BC, but even before this the work was well under way.

The forests of Germany were, and are, very varied in their composition. In the east and the south, pine and spruce trees are found in the greatest profusion, while in the west and in the Baltic uplands deciduous forest, especially beech, prevails. Among the Chauci and Frisii in the north-west, a mixed deciduous tree-cover was found. As well as densely wooded tracts, marshy ground and heathland cover considerable areas of Germany, Denmark and Holland. The heathland may in large measure be man's own creation rather than his natural opponent. Heath tends to develop from the degeneration of open woodland after the interference of human agricultural activities. Much of the heathland may, then, date from the Roman Iron Age. This is fairly clear in the case of some of the Danish heaths and those in central Holland. Here it is possible today to walk over land which is useless to the farmer, but which was once desirable for arable cultivation, as the visible remains of ancient field-boundaries make clear. Areas of marsh might be thought to be the last places where ancient settlers would attempt to make a living. But there were some marshy regions which offered excellent pasture for animals on their margins and these areas were colonised. The most important of these were the coastal marshlands of north Germany and Holland. Man's response to the demands of this kind of environment are worth more than a passing glance, as we will see (below, p. 39).

Our knowledge of the landscape inhabited by the early Germans is still patchy, since large-scale archaeological mapping of settlement areas has only recently begun. Archaeologists are now justly cautious about transferring to regions as yet unexplored the conditions and the settlement-pattern they have discovered elsewhere. The fullest of our information is about Angeln and Holstein, the homeland of the Angles who held this territory for centuries before their migration to eastern Britain in the fifth century AD. In Angeln the area settled by the German farmers was a combination of thin forest, in which they had cut a large number of clearings, and a parkland landscape dotted with copses and small clumps of trees, the result of linking up the clearings over a long period. The aim will not have been to remove all the tree-cover, for pigs and cattle could feed themselves for part of the year in woodland. It seems, then, that we should not take literally what the early literary sources say about the forested wastes of Germania. Certainly, there were large forests which were not settled at all during the period with which we are dealing. But in many regions man was master of his environment long before the first meeting of Roman and German.

LAND-TENURE

Information given by Roman historians helps us to construct some kind of framework for the early German system of land-tenure. There are, however, many difficulties involved in interpreting precisely what they have to say and still more in reconciling their accounts with the evidence of archaeology. The writers who tell us most are Julius Caesar, writing of the peoples he encountered east of the Rhine on his two brief visits, Tacitus, whose account is very different from Caesar's, and the fourth-century writer Ammianus Marcellinus, who offers our only considerable body of information about the German tribes at the time when the great migratory movements were beginning. It is greatly to be hoped that archaeology will one day fill out the meagre outline of this vital subject. Unfortunately, mute evidence from the ground will not help with the problems of who owned the land. Even complete excavation of settlements, though a mine of information on other matters, will not give the answers. Study of large areas of German settlement, followed by extensive excavation of the individual villages and farmsteads, will take us further along the road but that is work for the future. Meanwhile, the historians must be our source.

Among the Germans encountered by Caesar, private ownership of land was still quite unknown. 'No land is the property of private individuals and no-one is allowed to cultivate the same land for more than one year.' Caesar's picture is of a people equipped with elementary agricultural techniques, pursuing a type of farming which in essentials had remained unchanged from the time of the late Neolithic culture. The leading men in the community met each year to decide which parts of the land should be ploughed and planted. This area would then be parcelled out into equal plots and these were distributed among all the families making up that community. Next year, these plots of arable land would be temporarily abandoned to lie fallow and new areas would be parcelled out. Clearance of forest or scrub, ploughing and harvesting were normally carried out collectively by primitive communities and this is what Caesar is describing.

If this system were rigidly adhered to, and the products of agriculture fairly distributed among all the members of the community, it would be very difficult for one individual to raise himself above his neighbours in material resources and there would be no tendency for classes to develop within society. But is the picture drawn by Caesar a credible one? Even among peoples who had little knowledge of how to restore fertility to the land, the abandonment of their arable land regularly every year would not have been necessary. Moreover, in another part of his book, Caesar makes it clear that there were Germans who ordered their farming differently. The Menapii, for instance, dwelling about the delta of the Rhine, lived in isolated farmsteads as well as in villages, and the presence of isolated farms suggests individual rather than collective possession of land. There must be doubts, then, about the overall reliability of Caesar's statements. Further, what was true among the peoples whom Caesar encountered and heard of need not have been true of all the Germans. We will meet many indications of the private ownership of land at a slightly later time. Unfortunately, few actual settlements of Caesar's day and the period immediately following have yet been extensively excavated.

Writing a century and a half after Caesar, Tacitus reports in his *Germania* that the land to be worked in a given year, although still selected by the leading men, was parcelled out according to the standing of individuals in the community, with the leading men taking more desirable or bigger portions of the land than the rest. This passage in the *Germania* has been puzzled over more than any other part of the book. Such a process of land-distribution must have been very difficult to administer without creating endless feuds. A larger portion of land need not necessarily produce a crop larger than that grown on a small plot. The relative fertility of different plots of ground, farmed under fairly primitive conditions, would not always be judged to a nicety. Adjustments might have to be made in favour of the leading men after the total yield of the harvest was known.

However these problems were surmounted, it is clear that, by the time Tacitus wrote, private ownership of farm land was becoming accepted among the Germans. There are a few hints that this process began somewhat earlier. About AD 70, the great leader Civilis, who led a revolt of the German peoples on the lower Rhine against their Roman masters, possessed land and farms of his own near the Roman frontiers. It might be thought that since Civilis had imbibed deeply of Roman ways (he had served for a long time in the Roman army), his ideas on the owning of property were much more sophisticated than those of other Germans. But far to the north of the Roman frontiers, we will later be examining a settlement of this same time, where there are strong indications that a man of substance was calling the tune (below, p. 44).

The archaeological evidence, to which we can now turn, can make some useful suggestions on this matter of land-tenure, but can never be truly conclusive. By its means we can detect certain striking differences in size and character between dwellings in some of the settlements, and these differences are most simply interpreted as expressing differences of degree and wealth within the social order.

### THE SETTLEMENTS

Romans were struck by the great difference between the German settlements and those of the Celts. Germania could boast no town-like settlements to compare with the oppida of the Gauls and the Celtic inhabitants of central Europe. Still less was there anything in those lands which resembled a town in the Roman sense, or ours. 'Their habitations are isolated and scattered' is Tacitus' remark on the pattern of German settlement. How true is this? If they had no large settlements, what kind did they possess and what social units did these represent? The rest of this chapter explores the archaeological evidence.

Certain areas of northern Europe have produced an outstanding amount of information about the character of Germanic settlements, others none at all. The lower Rhine in Holland, Friesland and the north German coastlands, Denmark (especially Jutland) and southern Sweden offer the greatest concentration of known settlements and fortunately in these regions archaeologists have long appreciated the importance of placing man's settlement in its geographic and ecological context by studying the material remains against the background of climate, landscape and vegetation. These studies were pioneered on sites in northern Holland and thus the coastal area seems to be the appropriate starting-place.

## The Terpen

During the late Roman Iron Age, the sea began a long transgression of the coastline of Holland and northern Germany. From the late third century until about AD 650, continual inundations plagued the shore regions. Some idea of their devastating effect was felt quite recently in the same area, during the catastrophic floods of February 1953. As a result of the marine transgression in the Iron Age, the agricultural environment of the clay lands near the coast was drastically changed and the effects on the settlements themselves were equally profound. Instead of leaving the area and abandoning

*6 Distribution map of Terpen*

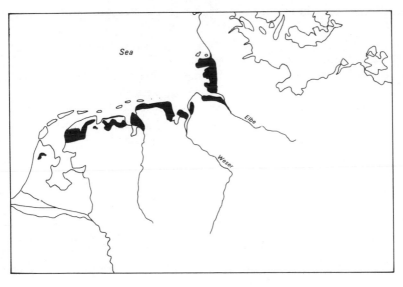

the rich pasture-land on the clays, the farmers dwelling there evolved a kind of settlement which could survive the worst of the flooding and around which a living could be made.

The solution they arrived at was the construction of artificial mounds on which the farm-buildings could be erected and to which the animals could be brought in time of flood. From the mouth of the Rhine to Schleswig-Holstein, the coast-line is studded with these dwelling-mounds, rising between six and twenty feet above the surrounding land. They occur not continuously but in close concentrations, as the map reveals. In Holland the mounds are known as *Terpen*, in Germany by a variety of names, of which *Wurt* is the commonest. Others are contained in the local place-names: *Werft*, *Warf*, and *Wierde*. The erection of the Terpen was due partly to the natural accumulation of occupation debris on the same spot over a lengthy period of time, but still more to the deliberate piling up of great dumps of animal dung and clay to provide broad platforms for the farms and their ancillary buildings. They vary considerably in size, from an acre or so to slight eminences on which only one or two buildings might be placed. Probably they inspired the description by the Elder Pliny of the dwellings of the Chauci, who held part of the German coastal region, as 'platforms raised up by hand'.

The Terpen do not all belong to the same period of time. Several groups or 'generations' can be distinguished. The earliest belong in origin to the early Iron Age, dating from the sixth century BC. The best known example of these early foundations is the Terp at Ezinge in Friesland (p.42), which continued under occupation for centuries. A second important group was founded early in the Roman Iron Age, beginning in the first century AD. Feddersen Wierde offers the most complete picture of a Terp dating from this period. Later generations of Terpen sprang up in the eighth century and even as late as the eleventh. A great number of the mounds still carry living villages on their tops, and in many of these cases it is possible that the sites have been continuously occupied since the Roman Iron Age or earlier.

Many Terpen have been severely damaged in modern times, others totally removed from the landscape. In the nineteenth and early twentieth century, the mounds were quarried

*7 A Friesland Terp, with the modern village of Hogebeintum occupying the mound*

for the ancient manure of which they were largely built up. During the wholesale destruction, enormous numbers of well-preserved objects were salvaged from the sites, little compensation for the loss of an important part of Holland's remoter past. Not until the Second World War was destruction halted and the remaining Terpen assured a future. Happily, in the past half century several have been skilfully and meticulously excavated.

The continual inundations of the low-lying ground and the consequent salination of the farmland might seem to have doomed agricultural prospects from the start in this region of German territory. But this is far from the case. The clay soil was, and remained, very fertile and cattle-rearing in particular flourished. Sheep too were kept, but they were overshadowed in importance by the cattle. Other domesticated animals included pigs, horses, goats, chickens and dogs. Fishing added something to the supply of food but the hunting of game appears hardly to have figured in the life of the inhabitants. Their life was above all else the life of pastoral farmers, for the extent of arable land was strictly limited. Some crops, however, were grown, including barley, wheat, flax, peas and beans.

The cattle-pastures spread widely around each Terp and beyond them lay the hay-meadows where, after the summer harvest, the young beasts were reared. The slopes of the mounds and a few of the higher lying deposits of silt *(houwen)* offered a little space for arable farming. In the peculiar conditions imposed by their situation, the Terpen land was probably owned by families and not by individuals. At least a certain amount of the precious pasture was held in common by different families in the village, we may imagine, and each family was also entitled to a number of cart-loads of hay cropped by the concerted effort of all the inhabitants.

Some of the most informative settlements ever excavated in Europe of any date are Terpen. Of their house-types and history, none have given fuller accounts of themselves than Ezinge and Feddersen Wierde.

## Ezinge

The earliest settlement at Ezinge, on the little river Hunze, consisted of a small group of wooden dwellings, two large farmhouses with living quarters at one end and a byre at the other, and a large rectangular building represented by nine rows of

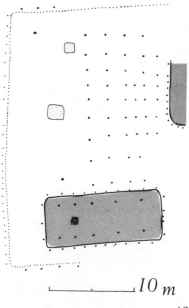

8 *The early farmstead at Ezinge (Friesland): about 500 BC*

10 m

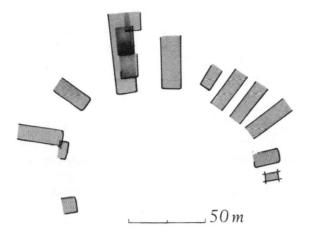

*9 A radially planned village at Ezinge: early Roman
Iron Age*

timber posts, five posts to each row, each upright being rammed
deep into the subsoil. Such a massive support for a timber
building implies that it was intended to contain something
weighty, probably on a raised floor. A granary is the most
likely identification, the raised floor being designed to keep the
grain away from damp and from vermin. The whole group of
buildings was enclosed by a timber fence or stockade and dated
from the sixth century BC. Like many other Terpen villages, the
successive settlements at Ezinge were almost all laid out on a
radial plan, the dwellings-cum-byres pointing towards the
centre of the village as spokes to a hub. The doors of the cattle
byres faced away from the houses towards a circular road, the
ox-road *(axwei)*, which ran round the perimeter of the settlement. At the heart of the village there would be a pond of
drinking water. The radial village-plan has never been abandoned in Holland and northern Germany. Some of the
modern hamlets on Terpen preserve the layout already
familiar to early Iron Age Germans.

The earliest occupation at Ezinge is firmly fixed in the sixth
century BC. During the pre-Roman and Roman Iron Age, a
sequence of four villages, consisting of small groups of farmhouses, occupied the mound. The settlements probably varied
in size, but they may be seen as communities of between five

43

and ten families. The latest of these four villages fell victim to a disastrous fire about AD 400, an event which left behind it a dense layer of ash and charcoal. Over the ruins a new settlement went up, but of so different a kind that the excavators of Ezinge believed that it had been established by the destroyers of the previous village. The houses were now of quite different character. The aisled buildings on a radial plan are gone, their place being taken by a large number of small pit-dwellings scattered in a haphazard fashion over the entire site. Apart from a very few pottery sherds which hint at imports from Gaul and even from the Mediterranean lands, the material associated with this phase of Ezinge's history consisted entirely of Anglo-Saxon bossed and incised pottery, most closely matched in the cemeteries about the mouths of the Elbe and Weser, and a few cruciform brooches from the same region. We may then be dealing with a settlement of Anglo-Saxons who migrated from their homes early in the fifth century and seized the site of a Frisian village after destroying it. It is equally likely, however, that the disaster which overtook the earlier village was of natural causes—a summer fire would rapidly consume a collection of timber and thatch structures—and that the subsequent inhabitants of Ezinge adopted a quite different life-style.

### Feddersen Wierde

Settlements in which a single dwelling dominates the scene are rare, but this is true of the most fully excavated Terp in northern Germany, Feddersen Wierde. Here the earlier hamlets are similar to those at Ezinge and the economic basis of life is still pastoral farming. During the first century AD, however, the planning of the settlement was drastically changed. A large aisled house, marked off with a fence and ditch, dominated the planning of the village, as no doubt its owner dominated social life. Around this dwelling lay a number of huts used as workshops, producing implements of wood, leather, iron and bronze. These workshops lay close to the 'great house' and were evidently under the control of the leading man of the community.

More than a limited degree of social organisation is implied by the size of Feddersen, by its evident self-sufficiency in metal-working and certain other crafts, and by its participation in

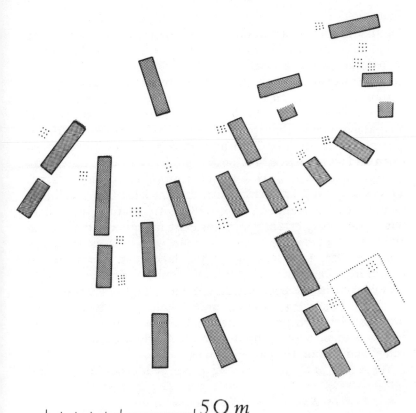

*10 The settlement at Feddersen Wierde (Wesermünde, Germany) in the third century AD*

long distance trade with the Roman Empire. Apart from the peasants who may have spent a limited part of their time pursuing crafts connected with the life of their farms, by the Roman period at least, a sector of the community seems to have been particularly concerned with iron- and bronze-working. Another unusual feature is that the peasants had at their disposal a large communal hall or meeting-place, perhaps provided by their headman. Not the least startling thing about the life of this community is its apparent stability. Not until the fifth century was there any interruption. Then came a marine inundation and the place did not revive until the early Middle Ages.

45

*Fochteloo*

Another residence of a man of some importance, or at any rate a man of means, can be glimpsed in a settlement at Fochteloo (Friesland), where a small farm of the first century AD centred upon a single aisled house has been completely excavated. The outbuildings were meagre in standing, amounting in all to three or four modest shacks, storebuildings and stalls. Immediately outside the house, a small area was parcelled out into plots of cultivated land and grass paddocks by means of wood and wattle fences. Five hundred yards away to the north-west lay a contemporary settlement of quite a different kind. This was a small hamlet consisting of at least two dwellings, together with associated stalls, wells, corn- and hay-bins. The two settlements certainly did not exist independently of each other. It is reasonable to see the man who lived in the large compact farm of Fochteloo as the landowner, drawing his wealth from herds of cattle, most of which were looked after by his followers in the nearby hamlet. The physical separation of the large house from the humble hamlet calls to mind the burial of richly equipped chiefs well away from the graves of common men, a phenomenon most clearly seen in the Elbe valley and among the east Germans.

We would not guess at villages like Feddersen Wierde and

*11  The Fochteloo (Friesland) homestead: first century AD*

46

*12 Cattle-stalls at Fochteloo*

Ezinge from what Tacitus says about German communities. He gives a picture of settlements which were rather loosely planned, whereas archaeology reveals developed villages. Nor does he mention the existence of larger houses which might belong to the leading men, such as are clearly visible at Fochteloo and Feddersen.

Ezinge and Feddersen were villages which, though frequently rebuilt, occupied the same site for several centuries. Another group of settlements has a quite different history. The site at Hamburg-Farmsen is a fairly fully examined example of this class. This village was occupied throughout the Roman Iron Age, but individual dwellings seem not to have stood for more than about a century. After falling into disuse, they were replaced by houses which might stand 50–100 yards away. The contrast between this shifting village plan and the almost static Terpen could not be greater. Possibly the Terpen were somewhat unusual in this respect, their static character being imposed by their situation.

*Palisaded settlements*

Another settlement which shifted over the course of time has been recently excavated at Grøntoft (Ringkøbing, in Jutland). In the third century BC this took the form of about six dwellings, all aligned in the same direction. All of these had stall divisions at one end. When this settlement was abandoned, it was replaced by another a short distance away, this one dating from the second and first centuries BC. It had five large houses of the usual aisled form, again aligned in roughly the same direction. But it differed from its predecessor in having a timber palisade around it, the whole enclosed area being about 100 by 30 yards. The palisade gives the appearance of a 'defended' settlement, but this is misleading. In reality it was no more than a strong fence to keep out wild animals rather than human enemies.

Similar fenced villages are those of Zeijen (Drenthe in central Holland) and the Bärhorst bei Nauen in Brandenburg (East Germany). Both of these were almost square in plan, with the internal buildings arranged on the same alignment as the boundaries. Zeijen was protected by a very stout timber palisade, perhaps strong enough to hold off attackers as well as keep out wolves. Immediately inside the palisade, the main dwellings and animal stalls were sited, thus leaving most of the central area of the settlement as an open space. This probably served one of the original functions of a village green, as a temporary pasture. The village at the Bärhorst was also surrounded

*13 Reconstruction of the Zeijen (Drenthe) village, early Roman Iron Age*

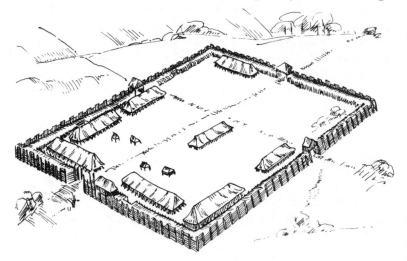

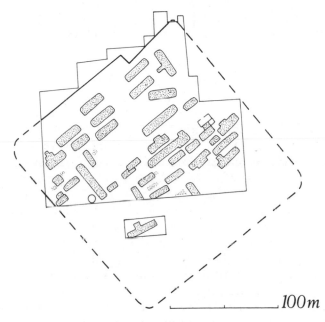

*14 The village at the Bärhorst bei Nauen, late Roman
Iron Age*

by a fence, but here the houses were set close together near the
centre of the enclosure, leaving only a small space in their
midst. Some 25–30 houses made up this village as against only
about eight at Zeijen.

Thus far, we have not encountered defended sites, with the
exception of the palisaded villages of Zeijen, Grøntoft and the
Bärhorst. In truth settlements with defences are rare in our
period. The best known case is the large village at Borremose
(Himmerland in Denmark). This lay on a small island in a
swamp, linked to the dry ground by a stone paved road.
Altogether 22 houses have been found on a space about 150 by
100 yards, but not all are of the same date. At one time some 18
houses were in existence. The village dates from the first century BC, but the defences which surrounded it—a rampart and
two ditches outside—belong to an earlier time. This is a community taking advantage of an earlier stronghold rather than
building its own refuge. All the houses at Borremose were
oriented in the same direction, and many had their ends

49

fronting on to a narrow paved street which ran through the interior to link with the road crossing the marsh.

## Wijster

The most intensively studied settlement site of the early Germans is that at Wijster, near Beilen in central Drenthe. Here, Dutch archaeologists carried out a most meticulous excavation from 1958–61, deploying all their highly developed skills in the study of the traces left by timber buildings. The result of their work is likely to remain for some time as the most complete picture we possess of the development of a settlement over a long period.

In broad terms the settlement was continuously occupied from the second century AD to the early fifth. In those three centuries there occurred remarkable changes in the layout of the place. The earliest settlement took the form of a single homestead housing one or two families. Around their dwellings lay outbuildings and sunken huts of the usual kinds. It may be that other farms like this one lay in the vicinity and that these family groups gradually drew together to form the village community which we find in the succeeding settlement phase. For in the next phase, a fairly large village came into being, in which the dwellings were roughly arranged in rows. Later still, this elementary planning becomes more marked. There was a clear break with the old buildings and a fresh start made with a larger number of dwellings and sunk huts. These occurred in closely set groups surrounded by timber palisades. The most striking of these groups, including some very large dwellings-cum-byres, lay at the heart of the village, arranged in a square. At least three other blocks of buildings existed, two of these separated from the central area by narrow streets or lanes. The impression conveyed is of an orderly settlement, carefully planned at the start and developing thereafter along lines that were foreseen.

As in other settlements of the early centuries AD, apart from the dwellings and sunken huts, the archaeological traces include granaries on wooden piles, large ovens or hearths set in pits, wells with wooden or wickerwork linings, and rectangular storage-pits lined with wicker and intended to hold grain and other food supplies. There are many instances of planning in

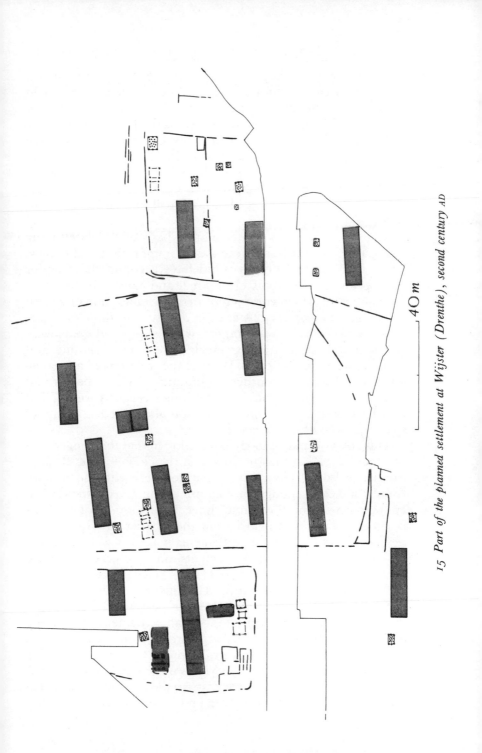

15 *Part of the planned settlement at Wijster (Drenthe), second century* AD

40 m

the siting of these ancillary features. Several of the stilted granaries lie close to individual dwellings, as though they held the grain-supplies of that one family. The storage-pits occur in groups, for example in two rows just inside the perimeter fence of the central block. And, as in many German villages, small groups of sunken huts lie close to a single dwelling, serving as outbuildings and working sheds. The Wijster houses themselves have many interesting features and one of the kinds of house represented, the cruck-buildings, we will look at later (below p. 70).

Mixed farming was the economic basis of this fascinating site. Cattle, as elsewhere, were the most important of the stock. Some of the largest houses could have accommodated 20 or more beasts. Horses too were reared, and eaten. Of the ritual animal burials which commemorated the foundation of several dwellings, those of horses were commoner than those of cattle. Pigs were kept in small numbers, while sheep and goats were either entirely absent or extremely rare. Since spinning and weaving were carried on at Wijster, the wool must have come by means of trade with other communities. Wheat, barley and flax were all grown, and probably other crops as well. What may have been a vegetable garden was also traced in groups of spade-marks within ditched plots.

This village is particularly interesting in that it belonged to a community of barbarians living fairly close to the Roman frontier of Lower Germany. Their contacts with the Roman Empire are clear enough in such minor things as pottery, glass and brooches, but there may have been more profound influences flowing northward from the frontier provinces. The regular layout of the later settlements may have been inspired by knowledge of Roman settlements, and the very size of the community—perhaps 500 people at its height—may be due to the influence of Roman standards of life upon its leading men. All the same, this large community of peasants did not go all the way towards developing an urban settlement. No public buildings existed and no fully organised trading economy was built up. Wijster does represent, however, the first stage in the development of a town and, as yet, is unique in free Germany. There is no doubt that its proximity to the frontiers, where real towns existed, explains its rather precocious growth.

SCANDINAVIAN SETTLEMENTS

So far, we have been considering mainly Holland and north Germany. What of Scandinavia? Literary sources say nothing about conditions here, but fortunately the results of skilled excavation in Denmark and Sweden have been generous and informative. Landscape and climate trammelled Iron Age man's way of life in Scandinavia much more severely than elsewhere in Europe. The long raw winters meant that cattle and other beasts had to be given adequate artificial shelters and thus well constructed, weather-proofed stalling occupied an enormously important place in the settlements of these regions. Perhaps more than any other single factor, provision of stalling will have led to a more fixed form of settlement than had existed in the preceding warmer periods of the Bronze Age, when animals could be left out in the open for nearly all the year. The need to provide winter fodder for stalled beasts inevitably resulted in the devising of better facilities for storing it. It is at this time, towards the end of the pre-Roman Iron Age, that traces of granaries and other food-stores make their first appearance. A further, and ultimately decisive, development in this close binding of man to single sites of habitation was the more intense cultivation of the available areas of ploughland, and a more concentrated effort to improve methods of growing crops.

Jutland and the island of Bornholm are the two Danish regions most fully documented. Certain Jutland settlements are nucleated villages, their houses arranged in rows and surrounded by fields. Skorbaek Hede and Osterbølle are the best known of these sites. At Osterbølle, the fields appear to be associated with individual homesteads and may thus have been privately rather than collectively owned and farmed. Bornholm, by way of contrast, was inhabited by farmers whose steadings stood singly in the fertile landscape. Down to the present day, there has been remarkably little movement towards the establishment of villages and village life on the island. Sites on Bornholm, notably Dalshøj, have produced good evidence for grain crops, principally oats, barley and emmer wheat, whereas the sandy soil of Jutland offered less opportunities to the arable farmer. Here, pastoralism, supplemented by fishing, played a much more prominent role.

_100m_

_16 The Migration period settlement at Vallhagar (Gotland), fifth–sixth
centuries_ AD

## Vallhagar

Further to the north-east, the Swedish island of Gotland boasts
the most informative of the known Scandinavian settlements,
Vallhagar. Here we have our first opportunity to study a
Migration period village in some detail. The 24 buildings
excavated on this site suggest the existence of five or six
separate farms, each of which comprised a dwelling and associated farm buildings. The social unit here represented is
probably a large group of interrelated families, each family
living on its own steading but combining for certain important
activities under the supervision of an elder. The clearance of
new ground for cultivation, ploughing and harvesting are the
kinds of task that would call out all their resources of manpower.

The economy of Vallhagar was based on mixed farming, in
which stock-rearing appears to have played a more prominent
role than the growing of cereals. The sea was only three
kilometres away but fish were not added to the diet. This is one
of the very few Migration period sites where the remains of
cereal seeds have survived in sufficient quantity to reveal clearly
what these Gotland farmers grew. The range of crops was wide:
six-rowed barley, einkorn, emmer wheat, spelt and rye were all
represented, with barley in the greatest quantity. Wild seeds
were also gathered and eaten, usually in a porridge. Flax and
cameline were cultivated, doubtless for their oil-producing
seeds. The total absence of oats is interesting, since it is well
attested in other parts of Scandinavia at this time.

The importance of stock-raising is revealed by the common-
ness in the pollen samples of wild plants characteristic of
meadows, such as buttercups, rib-wort and clover. But for
identification of the animals bred we are dependent upon study
of the rich finds of animal bones. Cattle and sheep were principally relied on but pigs and chickens also figured in the stock.
Herds of semi-wild russ horses were accessible to the inhabitants, the beasts fending for themselves in the surrounding
woodland for most of the time and being rounded up once a
year. Horse-meat seems to have been eaten in some quantity,
as at Wijster, and the number of animals over fifteen years of
age indicates use of the horse on the tasks of the farm. During
the winter the cattle were stalled indoors and fed on a diet of
hay. Some of the cows' milk was devoted to the making of

cheese, as may be deduced from the presence of bottle-shaped pottery strainers.

Vallhagar no doubt produced all its own food, but it was not an entirely self-sufficient society. Tools and pottery were obtained through trade with other areas of Scandinavia. Contacts with remoter lands are evidenced by the presence of glass drinking-vessels from the glass factories of Cologne and Vermand. Gotland is ideally situated to take advantage of commercial routes which ran north to south as well as those leading from west to east, and its inhabitants had plenty of agricultural products to offer in exchange for imports of pottery, glass and metalwork.

Vallhagar flourished in the period from about AD 400–550, and about the latter date came to a sudden end. Plentiful evidence for earlier farms beneath and to one side of the Migration period site suggests that the inhabitants were compelled to alter the position of their fields as the soil they tilled year after year became exhausted. The cultivated areas often occupied sloping ground, perhaps in the cause of good drainage, and continuous ploughing of such land, allied with natural erosive processes, could result in a thinning of the layer of humus. The relative smallness of the cultivated and wild seeds alike indicates that the ploughland was not of the highest quality. It may be, then, this part of Gotland could no longer support the kind of agriculture that was being practised. But whatever the real reason for the shifts in the siting of the farms during the Roman and post-Roman Iron Age, soil-impoverishment alone will not account for the ultimate abandonment of Vallhagar. The island of Gotland has produced a large number of hoards of Roman gold coins which abruptly terminate about or shortly before AD 550. This phenomenon, observable at different times in several parts of northern Germania, is best explained as the result of insecurity bred of war or incessant raiding, and it is against such a background that the last peasants will have left the site of Vallhagar.

MIGRATION PERIOD SETTLEMENTS

Excavated villages established in the Migration period are still rarities in all parts of western Europe. A few have recently been studied in England, but this phase of the settlement of the island is still remarkably little known. Villages of sunken huts are known at Cassington (Oxon.), Sutton Courtenay (Berks.) and Mucking (Essex), but that other buildings existed is made plain by the excavation of a village site at West Stow (Suffolk). Here a number of rectangular timber buildings, differing from their continental fellows in that they were not aisled, were accompanied by the ubiquitous sunken huts. The greatest gaps in our knowledge are those which concern Spain, Italy and France. From these countries, not a single well recorded settlement site has yet been published. We can only presume that, where the barbarian migrants established new settlements, they made them in the image of their villages in the homeland.

Even in Germany there has been little excavation of Migration period villages. For Frankish territory, we are still dependent upon the site of Gladbach, near Neuwied, for the clearest picture. This settlement was founded in the sixth century and comprised a large central dwelling-house, surrounded by many small sunk huts. The total number of buildings is about 50, and since most seem to have existed at the same time, a farly large village is in question.

In broad outline, the settlements of the Franks, Alamanni and Saxons were hardly different from those of the earlier Roman Iron Age and there were to be no great developments for several centuries. In the seventh and eighth century settlement at Warendorf near Münster, for example, we are seeing a large village which could easily belong to the fourth century AD.

The rarity of defended settlements in the Roman Iron Age has already been remarked on. In continental Germania they are equally rare later. In one particular area of Scandinavia, however, there is a great concentration of Migration period strongholds with powerful defences. This area comprises central and southern Sweden, and the Baltic islands of Gotland and Öland. The defences of these sites were commonly dry-stone perimeter walls thrown round a hill-top. Less often they were sited on level ground. Only a few are now well preserved, two of the best being Ismantorp and Eketorp on Öland.

Ismantorp is a circular fortress, 140 yards across, its defensive wall standing to a height of 15 feet in places. The interior has been meticulously planned, with stone walls radially arranged in relation to the defences to form no less than

*17 The fort at Eketorp (Öland), fifth–sixth centuries AD*

88 buildings. These lay in four blocks with streets between them. Despite the care and labour lavished on the layout of the place, few finds have been made in excavation here, and it may not have been occupied for long. Eketorp is another circular fort and here again we find the same radially planned stone buildings backing on to the defences. These distinctive structures have not yet been recorded outside Öland. Eketorp has so far produced the best evidence for the date of origin of these Scandinavian strongholds. The earliest material goes back to the fifth century, although occupation was sporadically continued until the Middle Ages.

These places are clearly not the settled peasant villages we have been considering in other regions. Plainly they are refuges for the local population in time of attack or unrest. The discovery of many hoards of gold objects on Gotland and Öland shows that these islands suffered a very disturbed period in the fifth and sixth centuries, and this must be the historical context for these striking places of refuge.

## TYPES OF SETTLEMENT

It will be obvious from this account that there is a great deal still to learn about early German settlements, especially about their economy and the development of individual sites over a long period. Their variety of planning is especially striking and prompts speculation as to the cause. At a later date, long after the migrations had ended, a number of distinct village types can be observed in northern Europe, the main criterion in their classification being the relationship of the houses to a central green or road. Can any of the early settlement types which we have been considering be the ancestors of these medieval communities? The case is 'non proven', but it is all the same interesting to look forward in time from the Migration period, seeking any sign of continuity in the forms of villages. The main types of settlement known in the early medieval period in the north of Europe are as follows.

1. *The Rundling*, in which homesteads are grouped in a ring about a central space. The doors of the outbuildings and the cattle-stalls face out towards the peripheral *axwei* or cattle-road. Among primitive agricultural communities outside Europe, settlements very similar in form are common.

2. The *Sackdorf* or *Sackgassendorf,* in which the buildings are arranged on an approximately rectangular lay-out on both sides of a street, one end of which is blocked.

3. The *Drubbel,* a loosely planned cluster of between four and ten homesteads about a central common pasture. Outside the village lay an area of common arable.

4. The Green-village, in which the houses are grouped around a green open space. This may be a broad rectangle or a narrow strip of ground on either side of a central street.

5. The *Haufendorf,* a loose agglomeration of dwellings in no orderly relationship with each other, but usually straggling along a street.

These village-types are seen in their developed form in the period after AD 1000, but the results of field-work give increasing support to the notion that several of them go back to the Migration period, and some further back still. The radially planned settlements at Ezinge, dating from the pre-Roman and Roman Iron Age, are evidently early *Rundlinge*. At Feddersen Wierde, a *Sackdorf* replaced a *Rundling* about AD 100 and at about the same time what looks like a green village existed at Zeijen, revealing that both round and rectangular settlement plans existed side by side in northern Germania.

We have shown that developed villages, and hence perhaps a developed community life, certainly existed in early Germany. These villages varied greatly in size from three or four families to 20–30 or more. But in several areas of Germania communities of this size probably did not exist at all. For instance, a considerable part of the population of certain Alamannic areas was scattered over many small hamlets of only two or three homesteads each. This conclusion was reached long ago on the basis of the small size of the cemeteries. Thus although villages of some size existed from the beginning of the Roman Iron Age at least, in some areas a proportion of the land may have been worked from isolated homesteads and small hamlets. And we must not forget that the village communities we have been looking at were not a sudden apparition. A Swedish scholar has put the truth of the matter succinctly: 'The organisation of German villages as communities was not created, fully developed, early in the history of those settlements. It is an end-product of a long process.'

AGRICULTURE

The settlements under review were those of subsistence farmers, and it is appropriate that we should end this chapter by considering some of the remains left behind by their farming activities. However brief the account of early German agriculture, it must not omit all reference to the important matter of field-systems. The fields which the archaeologist encounters in the vicinity of the settlements are of several kinds. Commonly they show up from the air as groups of irregular rectilinear enclosures lying at odd angles to each other, without any indication of overall planning. There is a close resemblance

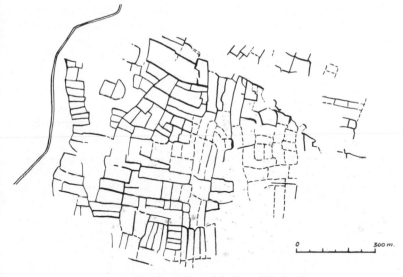

*18  Fields at Skorbaek Hede ( Jutland)*

here with the unhappily named 'Celtic' fields of prehistoric and Roman Britain. Well preserved groups of these fields can still be seen on the heathlands of Holland and in Jutland, their boundaries still marked by earth or stone walls. Quite frequently, regularly planned groups of squarish and rectangular fields appear, as at Skorbaek Hede (Denmark), at Zeijen (Holland) or at Fochteloo. At the last-named site, the excavators were able to define the home-closes and small fields near the settlement itself, these being marked off by wattle fences.

The fields of the late Roman and Migration periods have been less clearly revealed by archaeology, but they probably differed little from those of earlier days. Those at Vallhagar, for instance, are almost identical in layout with the small roughly rectangular fields of Jutland in the Roman Iron Age. Elsewhere in Sweden, and in Norway, the Migration period fields have been clearly identified and they are in the same tradition as the earlier. In the Low Countries and in the north German plain, rather longer narrower fields, superficially resembling the medieval strip-fields, have sometimes been assumed to go back to this time, but this has never been proved.

There is no basis for tracing open-field agriculture back to the sixth century. Indeed, it does not clearly manifest itself in Germany until the thirteenth century, so that the pervasive belief that common-fields were brought to Britain by Anglo-Saxon invaders in the sixth and seventh centuries must be discarded. They came into being through a long-drawn-out process which may not have begun until after the migrations were over. At all events, there is no trace of common-field agriculture as early as the Migration period itself.

The most important agricultural implement used in the fields was the plough. Its enormous significance is reflected in the fact that several examples have been found in votive deposits. Clearly it was held sacred as an instrument of fertility. In many parts of Europe the first ploughing was regarded as an act of sacral character as much as the start of another agricultural year. The plough had two forms in early northern Europe, the bow-ard and the crook-ard, ard being the Scandinavian term most commonly used for early forms of plough. The crook-ard is a very simple instrument, being in essence a hooked branch fitted to a long handle, to which in turn the traction animals would be yoked. The bow-ard is a more efficient tool, in that it has an arrow-shaped share fitted to the

*19, 20 Ploughs from Vebbestrup and Døstrup (Himmerland, Denmark), both about 500 BC*

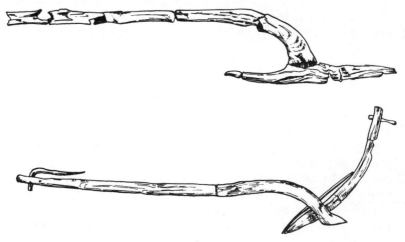

*21 Ploughing: a rock-engraving at Finntorp, late Bronze Age*

ard at an oblique angle, so that it turned the earth to one side when in use. It could also produce a deeper furrow than the scratch of the crook-ard. The still more advanced wheeled plough and the plough with an iron share seem to be later innovations, probably coming in after the Migration period.

The two examples illustrated both come from Himmerland (Denmark). The simple crook-ard from Vebbestrup, dating from about 500 BC has been formed from a single piece of birch wood. Its beam is slightly curved and measures more than four feet in length. The sole-piece is pointed at both ends, the sharper being the 'nose', since this served as the share. The 'heel' has a vertical hole or socket in it, into which a wooden stilt or handle was fitted.

The well preserved bow-ard from Døstrup is a larger and more sophisticated piece of carpentry. It consists of five carefully finished parts: a beam, a tie-piece mortised into the front end, a stilt fitted with a separate handle, and a fore-share. The beam, of alder wood, is about nine feet in length and tapers towards the front. The stilt and the share pass through a hole in its foot. This is heavily worn on the right-hand side, indicating that the plough has inclined in that direction when in use. While the beam is of hard alder wood, the stilt is of softer lime wood, and since it showed less sign of wear than the beam had probably been replaced at least once. The plough dates from the same time as that from Vebbestrup, about 500 BC, but both types of implement continued in use for centuries after this.

These simple wooden ploughs may not seem very effective instruments for dealing with heavy soils, and modern archaeolo-

*22  Wooden spade from Oostrum (Friesland)*

gists still frequently claim that the ard could only be used on light sand and gravel. This is by no means the truth and the falseness of the assumption has been demonstrated in a striking way. Beneath a number of Neolithic and Bronze Age burial mounds, traces of ancient furrows have been detected by excavators. These show up as discoloured stripes in the subsoil and they owe their preservation to the fact that the ground-surface into which they had been incised has been sealed off by the mound and thus protected against later ploughing and natural erosive processes. In a number of these cases, the soil into which the early ards had cut their furrows were heavy clays, showing that this land was by no means beyond the capabilities of the ard. Experiments on heavy land with modern replicas of the Iron Age plough tend to the same conclusion.

FURTHER READING

There are general accounts of settlement-types in O. Klindt-Jensen, *Denmark* (Thames & Hudson), M. Stenberger, *Sweden* (Thames & Hudson) and E. Oxenstierna, *The World of the Norsemen* (Weidenfeld & Nicolson). For Friesland, W. A. van Es, *Friesland in Roman Times* and H. Halbertsma, *The Frisian Kingdom* in *Berichten van de Rijksdienst voor het Oudheidkundig Bodemonderzoek* 1965–6 are useful. Technical excavation accounts of great importance are M. Stenberger, *Vallhagar* (Stockholm) and W. A. van Es, *Wijster: A Native Village beyond the Imperial Frontier* in *Palaeohistoria* (Groningen) 1965. A valuable study of ploughs and ploughing is P. V. Glob, *Ard og Plov i Nordens Oldtid* (with a long English summary).

# 4

# The Germans
# at home

For no other period of early European history are we so well
informed about dwellings as for the Roman Iron Age and
Migration period in Germania, particularly in Scandinavia,
north Germany and Holland. This is because a considerable
number of settlements have been extensively excavated and
also because in the Terpen and other settlements in marshy
surroundings houses and other buildings have in many cases
remained under wet or waterlogged conditions during the
intervening centuries. Thus, their excavators may find timber
and wattle walls preserved in almost pristine condition to a
height of three or four feet, offering an unusual richness of
detail to the student of timber buildings and their structural
techniques.

There are certain uniform elements which can be traced
throughout the history of early German houses. Two kinds of
building predominate, excluding almost all others: the aisled
house, or longhouse as it is frequently called, and the sunken
hut or *Grubenhaus*. The aisled house is a rectangular building,
divided longitudinally into a central 'hall' and two 'aisles' by
two parallel rows of timber uprights, usually with three or more
posts to each row. The aisles, or parts of them, are commonly
subdivided into small stalls for animals, especially cows, and
along the front of these there often runs a low rack of boards or
wickerwork designed to carry fodder. At the other end of the
building lay quarters for the family, normally a single large
room without any partition walls. Some aisled buildings were
built to house animals only, and were partitioned into stalls
along the entire length of their aisles.

*23 Reconstruction of aisled house at Einswarden*

In size there is enormous variation between buildings. The smallest measure, on average, 25–30 feet in length by 20 feet in width. The largest may be as long as 80 or 90 feet and up to 30 feet wide. This house type had a long history, the earliest European instances occurring in the Bronze Age. It first became common, however, during the early Iron Age. Long after the period of migration it was still being constructed in northern Europe. The essential form of this type of house was simple and invariable: hearth and home at one end, the stock and agricultural materials at the other. There were, however, many points of detail in which variation occurred—in the materials used for the walls, how the roof was supported, and where the entrances were sited. Some of these details will be apparent in the descriptions of aisled dwellings given below.

The other common type of early German building was the sunken hut or *Grubenhaus*, a simple timber structure erected over a shallow hollow dug into the ground. The superstructure comprised either a gabled framework of slanting poles tied to a ridge-pole, which was held aloft on two, four or six uprights, or a series of poles or branches sloping down to the edge of the hollow. Over this framework the walls were constructed, normally of wattle and daub, or planks. These huts, often only about 10 feet by 6 feet or less, were frequently employed as smiths' or potters' workshops, weaving-sheds, bakeries and the like, but they also served as dwellings. The plans of villages in northern Germania reveal them alongside aisled houses, and often associated with them, but settlements could consist entirely of *Grubenhäuser*, both here and in Britain.

A dwelling sunk into the ground might seem a crude form of housing, a hovel rather than a house. But not all *Grubenhäuser* were excessively primitive. The trim little building of about AD 400 at Emelang in Friesland shows a modest sophistication in the continuous foundation trenches for its walls and the low earth cladding against the wall-foot. For a reconstruction of the Emelang house, we may turn for aid to Frisian plank and turf houses of the eighteenth and nineteenth centuries, or the houses in the Drenthe paintings of van Gogh, the main difference being the presence of subdivisions in the modern dwellings. A common type of sunken hut is that with a little porch covering the doorway, like those at Gladbach. Others were entered down a little ramp or entrance-passage. In both cases, the aim must have been to cut off draughts through the doorway and to enable most of the outdoor mud to be kicked off the feet before entering the living-room. Sometimes a plank floor covered the hollow, the space beneath being used for storage or for the disposal of rubbish. The structure of the walls was very varied. Turf or earth dug out of the hollow could be used to build a low bank inside which the wall timbers were set. The uprights themselves were set either within the hollow or outside it. When placed inside, they were frequently two, four or six in number. In the two-post huts, the uprights supported a ridge-pole, in the others a simple raftered construction formed the roof.

Outside parts of Scandinavia, where timber well suited to house-construction is relatively scarce, the materials used were normally timber, wattle and daub, and thatch for the roof. It follows that only in waterlogged conditions will parts of such houses survive to the present day and even then we can expect to see only the lower parts of walls and the floor-levels. A

*24 Plan of house at Feddersen Wierde (Wesermünde, Germany)*

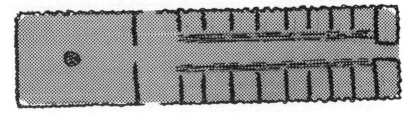

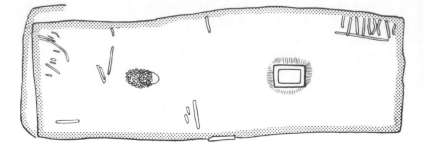

25 *Plan of house at Ginderup (Jutland)*

common type of aisled house is typified by those at Ezinge, Feddersen Wierde and Einswarden. In length the structure is normally at least twice the width and often more. The walls were of wattle woven about a framework of stakes, and they stood about six feet high. The stakes were embedded a foot or two into the earth and additional support for the walls was given by a number of sloping timbers ranged along the outside of the building. Two main beams held up on the internal uprights and perhaps tied together by short cross-members formed the roof support. The roof itself consisted of a series of poles fastened to the top of the walls at one end and to the roof

26 *Aisled house at Feddewen Wierde*

ridge at the other, and covered with thatch or turf. The corners of the house were often rounded, and the entrance lay in one of the longer sides, less commonly in the gable ends. The floors were usually beaten clay or earth. From settlement to settlement, house to house, there was great variation in the constructional details of walls and roofs but these examples of sturdy, well-built structures typify the dwellings of continental Germania.

In Sweden and Jutland the scarcity of timber meant that more emphasis was placed on stone and turf as building materials. The lower parts of the walls were in these regions built in dry-stone or turfwork, and the roof timbers rested on this solid base. The houses at Ginderup (Jutland), for instance, had turf walls originally several feet in height. The circumstance that some dwellings had been destroyed by fire while they were still standing and occupied preserved some constructional details not otherwise to be expected. Parts of the roof had collapsed on to the floor, its remains carbonised but still recognisable. It was shown to consist of a layer of thin rods with a covering of straw, this in turn being covered by another layer of heather and turf. Some of the wood and charcoal fragments from this and other settlements which went up in flames warn against underestimation of the skill of the peasant-carpenters. Large timbers seem to have been fitted tightly together with wooden pegs, some of them having been quite carefully trimmed and finished.

The stone-founded houses at Vallhagar illustrate a rather longer, narrower version of the basic aisled type, the dimensions being here dictated by the lack of lengths of timber of more than about 12 feet. As elsewhere, animals were housed under the same roof as the human occupants. The Vallhagar houses now seem stark and crude but once simple timber panelling may have concealed the roughness of the dry-stone walling and plain timber furniture will have made these peasant homes tolerably comfortable.

Although it is the commonest type of larger dwelling, the aisled longhouse does not stand alone. Rather smaller rectangular houses are known without any internal subdivisions. In these the weight of the roof was entirely supported upon the walls, which were braced externally to take the stress. There are

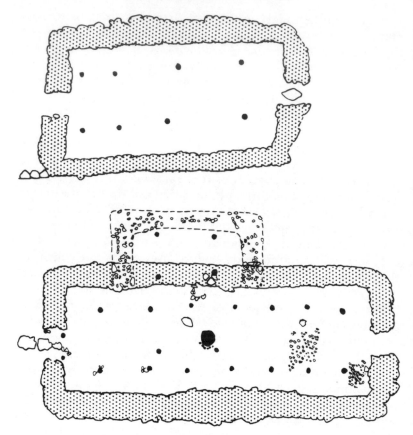

*27, 28  Houses at Vallhagar*

strong hints, too, that cruck-buildings existed in early Germany, though the detailed history of these cannot yet be worked out. In a cruck building, the roof rests mainly upon the upper parts of large curved timbers, or crucks, the bases of which were embedded in the ground just inside the line of the walls. Each pair of opposed crucks met at the roof-ridge. As yet only two early German sites, Westick bei Kamen and Wijster, have produced likely examples of cruck-houses and both date from the Roman Iron Age: Wijster from the first century AD and Westick from the third or fourth. The absence of this house-type from the other excavated settlements is striking, and the familiar cruck buildings of medieval Europe cannot yet be confidently traced back to an origin in barbarian Germania.

## FURNITURE

Knowledge of the internal fittings and furnishing of German homes is necessarily limited by the rarity with which individual pieces have survived, and by the fact that no Roman author seems to have interested himself in recording these details of barbarian everyday life. Most of the authors whose works have come down to us were in any case in no position to know anything about the interior of German houses. Tacitus makes no bones about what he regarded as the crudity of German houses and doubtless he believed that the furniture inside was no better and no more worthy of record. What we do know relates mainly to the higher ranks of society, being based on the richer grave-finds and a few votive offerings. It follows that the high quality of many of the surviving items was not common to all furniture. As usual, it is the domestic surroundings of the peasantry that have revealed little of themselves. These can only be guessed at.

Later saga literature often refers to benches, normally placed near to the walls of the house or hall, as the commonest form of seating, but single chairs were certainly known throughout our period and later. A very beautifully made little folding stool from a Bronze Age grave in Denmark, entirely constructed of wood but for its otterskin seat, was certainly paralleled in later centuries. A small chair from a richly furnished boy's grave beneath Cologne Cathedral gives us a glimpse of a piece of

*29 Bed and chair from boy's grave beneath Cologne Cathedral*

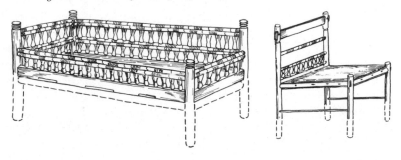

aristocratic Frankish furniture. This little chair is only two feet high. Its frame is entirely of wood and its seat of leather. The legs have been neatly turned and decorated with fine vertical grooves. The back is ornamented by a row of miniature balusters. This is a piece of unusually high craftsmanship, as befits the property of a boy-prince or chief. This grave also contained a little wooden bed or cot, likewise decorated with series of small balusters along the sides. Individual tables existed, being especially favoured by the warriors. In this respect, the German warrior resembled the heroes described by Homer and Celtic warrior-chiefs.

Richer homes may have had hangings or carpets, but of course these have hardly ever survived. A rare example of these comes from an elaborately furnished grave of a woman, also beneath Cologne Cathedral, but this is most probably an import from the eastern Mediterranean lands. Any German home outside the wealthiest circles would contain far less furniture than we would consider adequate, and probably only as much as many peasant homes in parts of central and eastern Europe today: beds, benches and possibly rugs of animal skins.

HOUSEHOLD UTENSILS

Household containers and utensils for the cooking and storage of food were made of pottery, bronze, iron and, not to be forgotten, of wood. The latter normally survive only in water-logged deposits in the Terpen and low-lying settlements, but the great variety of the known wooden vessels—buckets, dishes, platters, trays—reveals how important a material wood was in the German home. Bronze buckets, bowls, sieves and pans *(paterae)* were imported into Germania from the Roman provinces in great numbers and are frequently found buried with the dead, notably in northern Germany and in Denmark.

Fine vessels of silver crossed the frontiers to the same destination, as loot, as objects of trade, and as diplomatic gifts to German leaders, to be used in the banquets of the wealthier warriors and ultimately to grace their funeral rites. If as Tacitus asserted, the Germans held silver vessels as no more desirable than vessels of clay then it is remarkable that so many silver objects have come to light in Germania, and that this number includes some of the most beautiful and skilful products of their time. The enormous hoard of silverware found at Hildesheim near Hanover in 1868, consisting of some 70 items, may have been the fruit of a looting raid or raids on Roman forts or towns, and been later buried for the sake of safety, but many other finds of silver have come from richly furnished graves and have obviously been placed there as cherished objects, fit for a chieftain. The stream of silverware dried up long before the end of the Roman Iron Age, but imports of fine bronze vessels continued on a limited scale during the period of Migration, some of the items coming from as far afield as Egypt and the eastern Mediterranean.

Manufacture of pottery for domestic use was for the most part a localised craft over much of Germania. The great bulk of the pottery was hand-made, by the women of the community. The making of hand-made vessels in simple forms requires little technical skill and little preparation. Any fairly smooth clay could serve as the base, and after the pot had been brought to the required shape, a large fire on the domestic hearth would be enough to bake it to a satisfactory hardness. The range of shape and decorative treatment, even within a single region, might be considerable. For decoration, the potters of the Roman Iron Age resorted to a variety of simple techniques: combing, scored or impressed patterns arranged in panels, rouletting, finger-tip impressions, meander and chevron patterns, and occasionally appliqué ornament. As in so many

*30 Pottery from Altendorf
(Oberfranken, Germany)*

*31  Frankish and Alamannic pottery, fifth–sixth centuries AD*

other fields, the influence of the La Tène Celts is evident, both
in the shapes of vessels and in their decoration. This is particularly true in west and central Germany and in Denmark.
Imported Roman wares, both metalwork and pottery, also
served as models. The great mass of pottery which has been
recovered from this period, and from later times, has come from
cemeteries, not from settlements, and we must beware of the
assumption that the pottery in everyday use was normally
decorated. In fact, the grave-pottery in many areas appears to
have been specially prepared for its part in the burial rites. The
domestic pottery found in the settlement-sites is frequently
much simpler in form and commonly quite undecorated.

From the late Roman period onward there was an increased
emphasis upon stamped ornament in many areas. The finest of
these late Roman and Migration period stamped wares are
those found on the Baltic islands of Gotland and Bornholm.
Better known than these, however, are the vessels with stamped
ornament, frequently combined with bosses, found in the

region of the lower Elbe and Weser, the territories of the Saxons. It was by comparing pots with such decorative treatment from Stade on the lower Elbe with others found in East Anglia that J. M. Kemble in 1855 first demonstrated the archaeological evidence for a migration of Anglo-Saxons from the Elbe region into eastern Britain.

In other regions, other forms of decoration held sway. In Angeln, for instance, the Angles displayed a preference for grooves and dimpled ornament over stamped designs. Further east, incised chevrons and arcades were favoured. The Franks and the Alamanni used stamped and rouletted ornament freely, but their stamps were usually much smaller than those of the Saxons and much less exuberantly applied. Frankish vessel forms were from the fourth century greatly influenced by those of the late Roman pottery industry in northern Gaul and the Rhineland, but they brought into the Roman provinces several forms of their own. Characteristic forms are the deep, carinated bowls, with stamping on the upper part of the body, tall flasks or bottles, and shallow dishes or platters.

*32  Frankish glass: some typical forms*

*33 Drinking horn from boy's grave
beneath Cologne Cathedral*

A certain amount of wheel-made
pottery was produced by the early
Germans of the Roman Iron Age,
not all of it in regions near the
Roman frontiers. But wheel-turned
pottery in most areas played a secon-
dary role to the products of local
craftsmen and those who were responsible for the household chores.
Roman influence is often detectable
on German pottery, particularly on
the forms of vessels. This was due,
first and foremost, to the fact that
large quantities of good quality
Roman pottery were imported into
free Germany, especially during the
second and third centuries. German
potters also copied in clay the shapes
of imported metal and glass vessels.
After the settlement of barbarians
within Roman provinces in the late
fourth and fifth centuries, the Germanic traditions of pottery making
were in many areas greatly modified
by contact with Roman industries
which were still very lively. This was
particularly true of the Franks who
settled in the Rhineland and northern
Gaul. They found there Gallo-
Roman factories and workshops
turning out large quantities of domestic pottery. The techniques of production were kept going by the new
masters and the vessels reflect in
their new stamped ornament the
revised order of things. The forms
hark back to Roman predecessors.

In the early centuries, glass cups, beakers and bowls had been imported into free Germany from Rhenish factories and commonly were included among the grave-goods of wealthier barbarians. Under Frankish overlordship those factories continued to turn out good glass, especially drinking cups and beakers, in the fifth and sixth centuries. Often, these vessels have rounded bases and thus cannot have been stood upright on a table. Museum curators solve the problem by setting them in wire stands, but the alternatives facing the Frank were either to hold his glass in his hand between draughts or to drain the whole drink at one go. Another type of glass drinking vessel popular among the Germans was the drinking-horn, to our minds the most Germanic of utensils. From the first century AD, Roman craftsmen produced these vessels and exported them to the barbarian lands, where they mingled with their like in horn.

## FOOD AND DRINK

Classical accounts of what barbarians ate and drank tend to stress the differences between their diet and that of the Romans. So it is with Tacitus' sentences on German eating habits, and we have good reason to believe that he fails to give a complete picture. 'Their food is simple—wild fruits, fresh game and curdled milk.' The evidence from excavated settlements and from that macabre but fascinating source, the entrails of human corpses in northern peat-bogs, indicates that the truth is much more complicated.

The major role in German diet appears to have been taken by grain, especially barley and wheat, and various other kinds of seeds. As well as cultivated grain, wild seeds were collected and eaten, presumably from the same fields. The stomach and intestines of the famous Tollund Man provided an unusually detailed account of the doomed man's last meal, eaten and partially digested less than a day before he perished. The meal had consisted mainly of a gruel or thin porridge made from barley, linseed, knotweed along with other weeds which normally grow on cultivated ground. No meat or bone fragments were present. The stomach contents of other peat-bog corpses, for instance those from Borremose and Grauballe, also contained the remains of purely vegetarian meals consumed shortly before death. The man from Grauballe had dined off no less than 63 different kinds of grain and weed seeds. It is quite possible that the last meal of these victims of religious rites was sacrificial in character, but it need not have been altogether untypical of German diet in the north.

The evidence of animal bones from settlement sites reveals that meat did form part of the diet, though probably not an important one. Other animal products such as milk and cheese were consumed, cheese being attested by finds of cheese-presses from several sites. The presence of iron spits in some settlements suggests that some of the meat was roasted or grilled, and marrow was evidently popular to judge from the quantity of split bones. Game no doubt added some variety to the diet. At Vallhagar, aquatic birds including teals, mallard and guillemots were eaten and at Dalshøj seals were hunted, probably for their meat and fat as well as their skins. Fishing was practised on the Scandinavian islands and on the mainland coasts. Herring and sturgeon graced some tables at Dalshøj. In the second century AD, we even find Roman merchants with interests in Frisian fish, far beyond the frontiers.

The wild fruits offered by Germania at this time included the apple, plum, pear and possibly the cherry. Berries and nuts were plentiful. But the Germans seem to have been badly off for vegetables. Peas and beans were grown, but most of our modern vegetables are far removed by centuries of patient experiment from their wild ancestors. The use of herbs was appreciated and vegetable fats could be obtained from linseed and false flax.

As with other peoples of ancient Europe, salt was highly prized for its uses in preserving meat. War might be resorted to in asserting tribal rights over springs of brine. In AD 359, the Alamanni and the Burgundi did go to war on this issue. People living on or near the coasts frequently produced salt by evaporating brine in pottery containers.

Appropriately enough in the case of a people with an undying and well-earned reputation as topers, we know a good deal about German drinking habits. As among the Gauls and Iberians, beer was the favourite drink. This was brewed from barley and probably spiced with herbs. Apart from plain beer, drinks made from several ingredients reached the better furnished tables. One of the rich graves from Juellinge (Laaland) contained a bronze vessel in which traces remained of a drink fomented from several different kinds of berry. This sounds like a powerful fruit wine. Another grave, from Skrydstrup (Hadersleben, Denmark) contained two drinking horns. One retained the residue of a mead-like drink made from honey, and the other traces of beer. When we recall the great popularity of mead in later times and the relative ease with which it is made, it may be supposed that this was a common drink in the Roman Iron Age. Wine from the Roman world certainly came into Germania, though probably not in enormous quantity. Some of the very fine imported wine-sets, like that from Hoby, might therefore have been used as their Roman makers had intended. But one might hazard a guess that their barbarian possessor declined to follow the Roman practice of adding water to his wine.

## GAMES AND AMUSEMENTS

The Germans entertained themselves much as the Celtic peoples did, with feasting, music, dances and games of chance. One amusement which may have ranked as a spectator sport took the form of a dance, performed by the young men of a community, naked amid an array of swords and spears. By the first century AD, this seems to have been purely a sport, but it fairly certainly originated in a religious observance. Tacitus remarks that this was the only spectacle which the Germans put on, but this is unlikely to be literally true. A spear-dance is known from bronze plaques of the Migration period in Scandinavia and this may well have had its origins in the dances of which Tacitus had heard. Many other areas of ancient Europe have had their own sword and spear dances, a few of which survived into the medieval centuries. Contests of arms between young warriors probably formed part of their training for war, but boxing, wrestling and other athletic contests appear to have been unknown. Hunting too hardly ranked as an amusement so much as a means of supplementing the diet.

Archaeology tells us a little more about private amusements. Gambling with dice was a pastime which clearly found great favour with many, especially among the warriors of the retinues. The contents of the richer graves of the later Roman

Iron Age not infrequently include dice. These are identical to those of the Romans, the Celts and us, the numbers on opposing sides adding up to seven. No doubt the Germans picked up the game from the Celts of central Europe. Games played with counters on a chequered board were also known to the Elbe Germans and later to the Franks and Alamanni. Games on the ice in winter were also enjoyed. Bone skates have been found in several of the Terpen and another example comes from Vall-hagar. These resemble flat bone skates used until recently in Scandinavia and Iceland. Another winter game known to the early Germans and which was still played until the nineteenth century in northern Holland was skittles on ice. The skittles in this case were sets of the knuckle-bones of some large animal, usually a cow or a horse. These were knocked over by another lump of bone which was sent hurtling over the ice.

In general, however, organised sports and games occupied very little of a German's leisure time. Those who enjoyed more leisure than their fellows, the warriors, like the warrior-class in most primitive societies, spent it pleasurably and without exertion in drinking to excess, feasting their comrades, being feasted in turn, gaming, boasting and, throughout it all, quarrelling.

There are, however, hints of other, more creative pastimes. Interest in music is revealed by fairly common finds of small end-blown pipes of bone. Numbers of these have been found in the Terpen. They are difficult to date, but many must belong to the Roman and Migration periods. Some are no more than whistles, having no finger-holes pierced in the tube, but a few have as many as six holes so that simple tunes could have been

*34 Bone flutes from Frisian Terpen*

produced. Whether or not any of these instruments had reeds is not known. Stringed instruments can be safely presumed to have existed, although no actual specimens from the early centuries have been found. Two lyres were recovered from the late Alamannic cemetery at Oberflacht (Württemberg), one of them with six strings, the other possibly with eight. Another six-stringed lyre comes from a Frankish grave in the cemetery of St Severin at Cologne. These three finds are eighth century in date, but earlier musicians probably had similar instruments.

APPEARANCE

Roman writers commented freely upon the appearance of the Germans and their somewhat awe-struck remarks are richly supplemented by the many Greek and Roman sculptured reliefs, showing the Germans usually as opponents of Rome. But there is another source, which provides what is lacking for virtually all the other early European peoples, human specimens in the form of corpses preserved in peat-bogs. More than 400 of such finds have been reported in Scandinavia and northern Europe, most of them dating from between 100 BC and AD 500, when they can be dated at all. As we will see when discussing German religion, many of the people who died in the peat met their ends as sacrificial victims, others in expiation of crime. In several cases, the corpses are outstandingly well preserved, as is the case with the well known man from the Tollund bog, so that fine detail of the features is still visible.

The stereotype of a German in Roman eyes was a huge figure with powerful limbs, blue eyes and reddish or blonde hair. The great height of German warriors was always cause for comment in the German world and the skeletal remains in cemeteries of the Iron Age and Roman period do indicate a large-limbed, long-skulled population. Another feature remarked on by Romans was the fierce and terrible glance from their eyes, and this was commented on by much later German writers in the sagas. Almost all Mediterranean writers on the Germans mention their immense strength in the first onrush of battle, and their lack of staying-power if this did not produce results. The colour and dressing of their hair also earned special note. The red or blonde hair thought to be characteristically German, and incidentally greatly envied by fashionable Romans

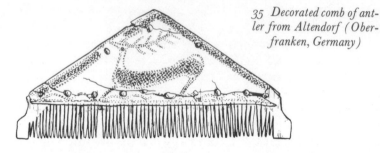

*35 Decorated comb of ant-
ler from Altendorf (Ober-
franken, Germany)*

male and female, was also greatly admired by the Germans
themselves. Some of those who did not possess it acquired it by
using a dye. When a band of German warriors was once sur-
prised by a Roman army in a riverside camp, some of the barbarians were drinking, others were bathing, and others were
busy dyeing their hair. For these warriors red hair was plainly
a sign of martial prowess. There is no good evidence that women
dyed their hair. Long hair, too, could hold a special significance. Warriors would let their hair grow as a sign that they
had undertaken a vow, not cutting it until the vow was paid.
Later, among the Franks, long hair was a special mark of
kingship.

Again, there were distinctive styles of wearing the hair.
Tollund Man himself had short cropped hair, but another male
corpse from the same peat-bog had a neatly plaited pig-tail.

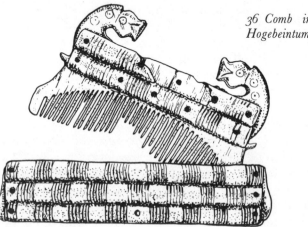

*36 Comb in case from
Hogebeintum (Friesland)*

37  *Face of the man from the Tollund bog (Jutland)*

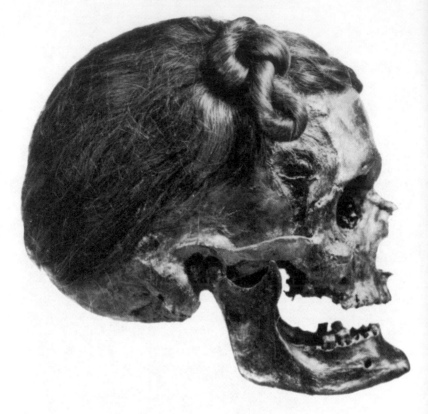

*38  Skull of man with 'Suebic' knot from Osterby (Schleswig)*

Freeborn members of the Suebian tribes, Tacitus tells us, affected a highly individual hair-style, the hair being gathered and tied into a knot, worn usually above or behind the right ear. This is confirmed by stone reliefs of German warriors and by a few corpses. Tacitus claimed that this knot served as a distinguishing mark for freeborn Suebi, but examples of the 'Suebic' knot have been found far outside the Elbe basin where those tribes were settled. The knot has never been noted on a female corpse or figure in a relief. Their hair is often shown as long and flowing, and when its colour survives on bog-corpses it appears as brown or fair, very rarely dark. The men commonly shaved their faces, as the frequent finds of razors testify, although moustaches and beards do frequently appear on the reliefs.

## CLOTHING

As with so much else, both literature and archaeology have more to say about the clothing of the wealthier members of society than of the rank and file. A versatile and apparently ubiquitous German garment in the Iron Age was the *sagum* or short cloak, worn by warriors in battle and by the peasant about his humdrum tasks. This was a simple rectangular woollen garment resembling a plaid, which might be wrapped round the body in bad weather, or used as a blanket at night, or worn thrown back over one or both shoulders. Usually it was fastened at the right shoulder by means of a metal *fibula* or brooch, or by a wooden fastening. Short, cape-like garments often made of animal skin are also commonly seen on Roman representations of Germans and on peat-bog corpses. These

*39   German   prisoners wearing short capes, from a   Roman   monument   at Mainz (Germany)*

covered no more than the shoulders and the breast, the rest of the body being often left bare. Other garments in common use among the men, judging from bog-finds and Roman reliefs, were trousers and a shirt-like tunic. Both of these tended to be close-fitting, suiting well their use in the northern winters.

Trousers make their first appearance in the northern peat-bogs about the end of the first century BC, and may have been brought into northern Europe by contact between the Germans and steppe nomads far to the east, who spent a large part of their days on horseback. This was not, however, a distinctively German garment. The Celts, and incidentally the Chinese, derived their use of trousers from the same nomadic source as the Germans. The actual specimens which have been recovered from the peat show great variety of design. Some are merely short breeches reaching only to the knee. Others cover the lower legs as well, and one pair even has covering for the feet. On Roman monuments Germans often appear wearing trousers and nothing else. When the upper parts of the body were to be covered, a tunic, usually of wool, was donned. This tunic could be with or without arms, and reached down to the waist or hips. Shoes of sheepskin or hide are occasionally found, and in areas fairly near the Roman frontiers shoes of good leather were worn. Elsewhere, leather footwear was something of a luxury.

Animal skins as well as woollen garments figured in the German wardrobe, especially those of lambs, sheep and cattle. Wolf- and deer-skins, and possibly bear-skins as well, were much more rarely used. Usually the skins were made up into simple trapeze-shaped garments and not simply worn as one-piece skins. Oddly enough, although Tacitus specifically mentions the use of the pelts of sea-creatures, obviously seals, among the Germans, none have yet been found either in graves or waterlogged deposits. Some Germans of the Migration period, Goths and Franks among others, appeared to their Roman adversaries as wearers of skins, but they possessed woven clothing as well. Animal hair was occasionally used in combination with wool, being woven into the textile together with the yarn.

The quality of most of the surviving garments is uniformly high and a few are outstanding products of the weaver's art,

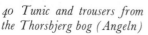

40 *Tunic and trousers from*
*the Thorsbjerg bog (Angeln)*

41 *Woman's dress from*
*Huldremose (Djursland,*
*Denmark)*

revealing advanced techniques and a high competence in their
execution. Dyeing and patterning were practised. A garment
from the Thorsbjerg bog had been dyed an indigo colour. At
the settlement of Ginderup (Jutland), a vessel was found to
contain a vegetable dye which had been intended to produce
blue colouring for textiles. Apart from wool and skins, linen
may have been used for finer pieces of clothing. Unfortunately,
linen does not survive in waterlogged peat so that no actual
remains can be studied.

As we saw, male attire seems to have consisted mainly of the *sagum*, the cape, trousers or breeches, the tunic and, at least occasionally, shoes. What of German women's dress? Tacitus gives the impression that they wore the same kinds of garment as the men, except that they went in for linen underwear and left the upper parts of the breast and arms uncovered. This is misleading. There is no evidence that women ever wore trousers. Whenever trousers have been found associated with a corpse in the peat, the corpse has been that of a man. When clothed female corpses have been recovered from the peat, their dress usually differed markedly from that of the men. Woollen skirts of various lengths are the commonest single garment.

The fullest picture of women's dress in the Iron Age is provided by two outfits from Huldremose in Denmark. One lady had two skin capes of the usual pattern, a woven skirt and a scarf or shawl fastened together with a bone pin. The skirt was patterned in a squared design, produced by using two different coloured yarns, one dark brown, the other a lighter shade. The other outfit found nearby was of quite a different kind. This was a one-piece dress, extending from the shoulders to the feet. Its shape was sack-like, but careful arrangement and gathering at the shoulder and waist could make it an attractive as well as a versatile garment. A large fold could be left behind the neck to form a hood in cold or wet weather. In form this dress is very similar to the *peplos* worn by Greek women in the fifth century BC. Perhaps it came from a common Indo-European source. That it was a fairly common attire in Germany is apparent from the reliefs on the column of Marcus Aurelius in Rome, on which many barbarian women are depicted wearing dresses of this kind.

Ornaments worn on the dress by both sexes were fairly simple during most of the Roman period. The commonest ornament was the *fibula* or brooch, a functional object used to gather together folds of cloth or to hold two garments together. The brooches of the earlier Roman Iron Age were usually of iron or bronze. Their shapes reveal much borrowing from the Celtic lands. Common types are the angular and sharply involuted forms, both of which were originally imported from central Europe. Later there was free borrowing of Roman brooch-types and import of actual Roman brooches. In the

*42 Brooch from Huizum
(Friesland)*

*43 Bow-brooch from
Friesland*

late third and fourth century, Roman crossbow- and onion-headed brooches crossed the frontiers into Germania, there to influence profoundly the development of Germanic brooch-types.

Like the brooches, the other ornaments were only occasionally splendid pieces. The fine girdle-chain of the first century BC from Swichum in Friesland is a rarity. The usual adornments were bracelets of bronze with simple decoration, pins with knobbed- or ring-heads, and bead-necklaces. Some of the men wore belts with handsome bronze buckles and various other ornaments. This picture of plainness was drastically altered during the fourth century, and in the Migration period barbarian chiefs and their followers decked themselves

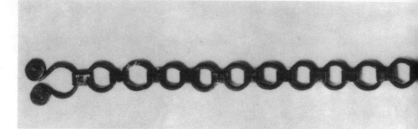

*44 Girdle from Swichum (Friesland)*

out with some of the most splendid jewellery Europe has ever seen.

The dress-ornaments and decorative items for the person, particularly the brooches, were conspicuous features of attire. The brooches were practical objects, performing the necessary function of fastening garments together and holding cloaks in position, but they were also worn in prominent places on the shoulder or the breast and so were worthy of rich decorative treatment. The brooches range from very simple forms with crude decoration to sumptuous gold objects with delicate ornament or inset precious stones. The range covers every social degree from peasant to war-leader. Probably they were more than sub-conscious signs of rank and prestige. The more expensive and handsome the ornaments, the more powerful their wearer. But they were more than status-symbols. At the head of the social scale, the kings and war-leaders had to reward their followers with costly objects, rings, brooches, collars and the like. The wearing of such things by the king or noble himself would therefore be expected as a necessary advertisement of his prestige and guarantee of his power to repay services. In a society which did not know the motor car or the private aircraft, symbols of prestige could best be provided by personal adornments and fine weapons.

The leading class of brooches of the Migration period was the bow-brooch, a type with a long ancestry reaching back to the pre-Roman Iron Age. It consisted of a bow-shaped piece of metal linking two flat plates, one at the head, the other at the foot. The functional pin was anchored to a spring behind the head and, when in position on a garment, was held in a catch-plate behind the foot. Variants of the basic form were numerous.

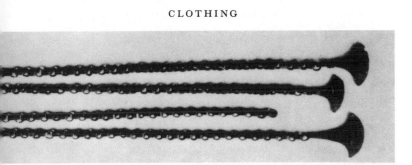

The simplest was the cruciform brooch, which had a cross-shaped head and a foot usually decorated with a stylised animal head. In the fifth century, notably in Jutland, the cruciform head was sometimes replaced by a rectangular plate covered with animal- and scroll-ornament the square-headed brooch. As time went on, the heads, feet and even the bows became still broader, and in the finer specimens were covered with intricate stylised animal ornament. From the fifth to the seventh century

45 *Frankish brooch from Herpes (Charente)*

46 *Equal-armed brooch from Haslingfield (Cambs.)*

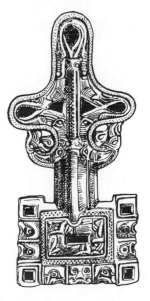

47 *Bird brooch of Frankish type from Chessel Down (Isle of Wight)*

AD, these bow-brooches were current all over western Europe. Then they began to give way to disc-brooches, particularly among the Franks, Alamanni and Lombards.

Another member of the family of bow-brooches was the equal-armed brooch. In this form, a fold of cloth could be held up in the upper part of the brooch while the pin passed through it. The distinctive character of this form is given by the broad, lateral spread of head and foot. These parts of the brooch often bear spiral ornament and flowing animal shapes much influenced by the work of provincial Roman craftsmen. The equal-armed brooch belonged to the fifth century and it was at home in the Saxon lands of north-west Germany. Rather commoner and belonging to the same period of time is the circular saucer-brooch. This normally bears a decoration of chip-carved spirals.

A much more widely spread type was the brooch in the form of a bird of prey. The finest examples form a richly ornamented series inlaid with garnet cloisonné. The most splendid pieces of this class were worn by Goths and Lombards in Italy but the type was also known to the Franks and Alamanni.

This bird-motif came to the Germans ultimately from the steppe-nomads, probably with the Huns as intermediaries. Another form which was derived from the art of the nomads was the brooch in the form of a horse and rider. A fine example is a sixth century brooch from Xanten on the lower Rhine. This is of silver with gilding on its surface and shows a helmeted warrior on a galloping horse. Though horse and rider are badly out of scale, the figures have a good deal of lively movement.

Amidst all these fairly elaborate brooches, simple forms still circulated. The most persistent is the little pennanular or annular brooch, a plain ring with a pin crossing it. There were many variants of the main form. An interesting variant of the annular brooch occurs among the Alamanni and in Frisia. This has a slot for the pin and about the slot the brooch is ornamented by animal heads or incised decoration.

Many other kinds of ornaments were worn by the well-to-do Germanic ladies. From finds of their graves it is possible to build up a full picture of the contents of their jewel-boxes. Their belts or girdles often had ornamental components and

 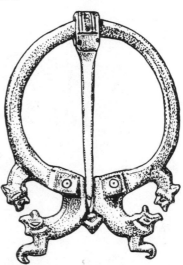

*48 Horseman brooch from Xan-
ten (Germany)*

*49 Annular brooch from Fries-
land*

other decorative pieces hung from it. The buckle might be of
solid gold or silver, and the strap-ends and belt-mounts of the
same metal. Beads or glass ornaments might be fixed to it and
occasionally balls of crystal with gold or bronze mountings
hung from it. These were possibly amulets with magical powers
rather than ornaments pure and simple. Necklaces were very
varied. The finest were gold and silver chains with gold
pendants, often old Roman coins, hanging from it. Others
were of wire with bronze pendants and glass beads, and the
commonest of all were made up of large glass beads only.
Bracelets, too, were of many kinds, ranging from twisted bronze
wire to solid gold pennanular rings with thickened terminals.
These, and finger-rings, were worn by men as well as women.
Ear-rings at their finest could be very elaborate. The most
splendid had large loops of gold wire which passed through the
lobes of the ear, and hanging from the loops were heavy gold
ornaments, often ornamented with filigree and with inset
garnets or glass. Rather similar massive ornaments were placed
at the heads of silver and gold hair-pins.

The most significant development of the fifth century was the
introduction into the West from the Black Sea regions of the

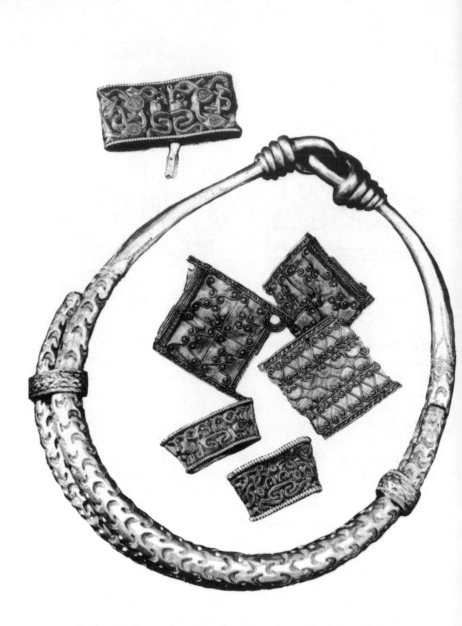

*50 Gold neck-ring and scabbard mounts from Tureholm (Södermanland, Sweden)*

'polychrome-style' of jewellery. Gold brooches and other ornaments, heavily encrusted with precious and semi-precious stones, garnets, and glass, rapidly increased in popularity, until by the seventh century they had become the dominant element in Frankish jewellery. This polychrome ornament was to be the most abiding legacy of barbarian craftsmen, for it set the fashion for the finest jewel-work until the Ottonians.

The most elaborate of all ornaments were the massive gold neck-rings, or torcs, and collars favoured by the wealthy inhabitants of southern Sweden and the Baltic islands of Gotland and Öland. These first appeared in the late Roman period but they reached their splendid peak in the later fifth and sixth centuries. Pride of place goes to the superb collars from Färjestaden, Möne Kirche and Ålleberg, and the torc from Tureholm. Sweden boasts a truly astonishing array of gold from this period. As well as the collars, there have been many finds of gold spiral arm-rings, bracelets, and massive finger-rings of gold, often set with large semi-precious stones.

The Scandinavian 'Golden Age' jewellers acquired their gold not from local sources but from the Roman world, probably in the form of gold coins *(solidi)*. Numbers of hoards of such coins have been found on Gotland, Öland and Bornholm. Some idea of the great wealth centred on Scandinavia in this period can be gained by converting one of the gold hoards, that from Tureholm, into Roman solidi. This single hoard represents some 3,000 *solidi*, not a huge fortune, but a handsome sum when we consider that captured Roman soldiers could be bought back by the Empire for only 8 solidi each.

## FURTHER READING

A recent survey of this subject is B. Trier, *Das Haus in Nord-West Europa* (Münster). The works noted at the end of Chapter 3 also contain descriptions of the main house types. To these might be added, C. A. R. Radford, *The Saxon House: A Review and some Parallels* in *Medieval Archaeology* 1957. P. V. Glob, *The Bog People* (Faber) is a good summary of the plentiful information derived from Danish peat-bogs about physical characteristics and attire.

# 5

# Weapons and
warfare

## THE ROMAN PERIOD

After the stabilisation of the Roman frontier on the Rhine early in the first century AD, there was little serious threat to the northern defences of the Empire for many decades. It was not until the third century that this frontier began to creak alarmingly under the weight of barbarian pressure. By this time there had occurred an important regrouping of barbarian tribes, a development which contributed to the passing of military initiative from the Imperial forces to the Germans. In the main, German attacks were strikes against weak points in the frontiers, often when Roman attention was focused elsewhere. Set battles against a well-equipped and highly trained Roman enemy were avoided, and that there was reason for this will be clear as we proceed. The greatest difficulties faced by the Roman armies during the prolonged and arduous campaigns in Germany between about 58 BC and AD 15 were the difficulties presented by the terrain of forest and swamp, rather than the opportunist German tactics which that terrain encouraged.

In virtually all the departments of war indeed, the Germans were outclassed by their Roman opponents. In strategy, in the tactics of close-order fighting, in training, in the weapons they carried, in the organisation of defended strong-points and camps, and in the provision of supplies, the Germans of the early Imperial period stood in the same technical relationship to the Roman army as the hosts of Matabele and Zulu to the nineteenth-century armies of Britain. The invader could be crushed, but only if taken by surprise. In a set battle, his technical superiority ensured his eventual triumph. Nevertheless, the German warrior was feared, for had not his spirit and strength inflicted two of the most humiliating defeats upon the Roman state? The disasters in the Rhone valley in 107 and 105 BC, and in the Teutoberg forest in AD 9, were terrifying enough to account for the contemporary Roman respect paid to the German fighting man, but even contemporary Romans must have been aware that in both these cases the result was predetermined by the incompetence of Roman generals, and owed little to German military skill.

At the outset it must be stressed that at no date was the German art of war homogeneous. Even in the early Roman Iron Age, for which period we have Tacitus' *Germania* as our guide, appreciable differences in weapons and tactics can be discerned between tribes or other folk-units. Literary sources for the Migration period tell a similar story. Care is needed therefore in attributing particular customs and items of war-equipment to the various Germanic peoples. In the absence of specific literary or archaeological testimony, no assumptions about the use of a particular weapon, or method of fighting, among any group of Germans can be made. A further factor which brings complication is the uneven distribution of our evidence over the peoples of Germania. The literary sources cover, for the most part, the tribes living close to the Roman frontiers. The results of archaeological research also do not reveal the material culture of all the Germans to the same depth. Certain areas, for instance parts of Scandinavia and the Elbe-Weser region, have been thoroughly worked over by archaeologists, while others are almost complete blanks.

Alerted to some of the main difficulties, we can pick our way along a path for which Caesar and Tacitus provide the sign-posts, but the course of which must continually be checked against the finds of actual weapons.

## CAVALRY AND INFANTRY

The mass of German warriors at this time fought on foot. Large numbers of cavalry were quite unknown, and only chiefs and their retinues seem to have been able to afford horses and their upkeep. To what extent even these limited cavalry forces were an effective fighting arm is a point not yet clarified. There are some historical accounts which place the German mounted

97

men higher in the order of merit than the infantry, and it is true that Germans could be converted into skilled cavalrymen. The horsemen of at least one tribe, the Batavi of the lower Rhine, provided several reputable regiments of cavalry for the Imperial army of the first century AD. Probably German cavalry would have left a more permanent impression if more warriors had had the means to maintain a horse and its equipment. Apart from the Batavi, another lower Rhenish tribe, the Tencteri, excelled in the arts of horsemanship and in fighting from horseback.

Among these people, skill in riding was the aim of children at play and of youths in training. The bequest of horses on the death of the head of a household was governed by special conditions. The bulk of his possessions passed to the eldest of his sons, but the horses were destined for the son who had shown himself the best fighting man. But the Tencteri earn the special attention of Tacitus, to whom we owe this information, because their devotion to cavalry warfare was matched by no other tribe known to him. Apart from the sandy heath-lands of the lower Rhine, and the plains bordering the North Sea, it is difficult to point out areas where large cavalry forces can have acted to good effect, and this may go some way towards explaining why development was slow in this branch.

In Roman eyes, German horses were distinguished neither by their shape nor their speed. On one occasion at least, Caesar remounted his German auxiliary troops on Roman horses, as their own were not suitable. Since the cavalry was composed of the wealthier warriors of the chiefs' retinues, the horsemen tended to form a social and military élite. Little is known of cavalry tactics. A German speciality which must have disconcerted Roman infantry on first acquaintance was to place a number of warriors, selected for their fleetness of foot, among the cavalry lines. These commando-like infantry kept pace with mounted troops and aimed at adding to the confusion caused by the shock of the cavalry rush. The mounted troops were armed mainly with lances, but at least a proportion were equipped with swords. Where swords have occurred in grave-finds, they have frequently been accompanied by horse-gear. The bow and arrow hardly figures at all before the third century AD, and even then was not a common weapon.

## WEAPONS AND ARMOUR

Archaeological evidence accords completely with the statement of Tacitus that early German warriors were normally armed with a lance *(framea)*. This was commonly no more than a stick of ash-wood, its pointed end hardened by fire, but it was often equipped with a bone or iron head of varying length. Some of the Germans who faced the invading Roman legions carried lances with exceptionally long heads, the sight of which so terrified the legionaries that their general had to persuade his men that only the enemy front rank carried such destructive weapons. Well before the end of the Roman period, these long spear-heads had been abandoned. A number of lances might be carried into battle by each warrior, to be used either as throwing or thrusting weapons, as occasion demanded. The spear and the shield were clearly the principal German battle equipment at this time. It was with these that the young warrior was arrayed by a chief or a kinsman when he had reached manhood, and was consequently allowed the privilege of bearing arms.

The sword played a relatively minor role in Germanic warfare before the late Roman period, and even after that time it hardly ranked as the weapon of the common man. Centuries were to elapse before fine Frankish blades were to be highly prized by Viking soldiers, but from the third and fourth centuries AD blades of excellent quality begin to make an appearance in Scandinavia and northern Germany (p. 116). The one-edged slashing blades of the pre-Roman Iron Age were gradually replaced by two-edged swords, but the introduction of this more versatile weapon was not accompanied by any significant increase in the number of sword-bearing warriors.

Several weapons from Scandinavia and from regions nearer the Roman frontiers on the Rhine and Danube are close enough

*51 Sword of* gladius *type from Stenstuger (Gotland)*

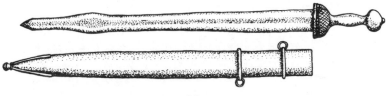

to the Roman short sword, the *gladius,* to suggest derivation from the legionary weapon. Their prototypes, too, distinguishable as Roman by their shape and occasionally by the presence of makers' name-stamps, occur in small numbers beyond the frontiers, and doubtless made their way there as objects of loot or illicit trade. Their presence in the great votive deposits of smashed and slighted equipment, Roman and German alike, hurled as offerings to the gods of war into marshes, suggests that rather more Roman gear accrued to the Germans as the spoils of war than through 'gun-running' across the frontier (p. 124).

By the fourth century AD, most swordsmen, Roman and German, were carrying a long, slashing weapon of Celtic origin, the *spatha.* Some examples of this type of sword were highly skilled products of the pattern-welding forging process (p. 116). The adoption of the *spatha* by Roman troops is merely one aspect of a long process of the 'Germanisation' of Roman arms and equipment, as more and more barbarians were drawn into the Imperial service on the frontiers. This is most strikingly evidenced by the adaptation of Roman military metalwork to art-styles favoured by Germans.

Another sword type of the later Roman period was a long

52 *Wooden shields from Hjortspring peat-bog (Als, Denmark)*

rapier-like weapon with a narrow, flexible blade, very reminiscent of medieval fencing weapons. Like the *spatha* this type
of sword was being used by both German and Roman troops,
and its origins lay in the Empire.

The main means of defence was the shield. This was often a
rectangular or round wickerwork or wooden framework,
strengthened by leather mountings and an iron binding round
the rim, and usually carrying a prominent wooden or iron boss.
Roman triumphal sculpture quite commonly shows oval, rectangular and sexagonal German shields, types which sculptors
also associated with the Gauls. Probably the rectangular and
sexagonal shields are another result of German contact with the
Celtic lands of central Europe. The common round shields,
actual specimens of which have come from the Thorsbjerg and
Vimose bog-deposits, measure about one metre in diameter.
Attempts to link these exclusively with cavalry, and the larger
rectangular shields with infantry, have foundered. The outer
surface might be painted so that men from different units or
tribes could be easily distinguished.

The inherent weakness of the German shield meant that it
could not be employed simply to cover the vital parts of the
body, like the Roman *scutum*. It had to be used away from the
body as much as possible, deflecting missiles and parrying
blows rather than merely stopping them in their onrush. The
boss added to the shield a limited function as a thrusting weapon
as well as a deflector of enemy blows. The skilful wielder could
also twist it so as to force the sword or lance from an opponent's
hand.

Body armour at this date was rare, and probably only chiefs
rose to it. The rank and file entered battle naked or clad only in
a cloak, or in trousers. Some chiefs wore garments of leather
over the upper parts of the body, but even this modest protection was exceptional. Probably rarer still were garments of
rivetted chain-mail. These are so far confined to small areas of
northern Germany, the lower Elbe and Jutland. Further instances come from Öremolla (Skåne, southern Sweden) and
from Granby in Uppland. The most remarkable group of mail
coats is that from the Hjortspring bog deposit, a large repository
of war-gear dating from 200 BC. Here no less than 20 garments of
mail or parts of them were found. Where this armour came from

is unknown. The Celtic lands in central or western Europe are one possibility, the Roman Empire is another.

Helmets of Roman date are equally rare and probably served as insignia of rank as much as protective gear. Occasionally, Roman helmets might be imported. A cavalry helmet from the Thorsbjerg bog in Schleswig had been modified by a German craftsman, who weakened it by stripping away some of the metal. Like the chieftain's helm from Hagenow in Mecklenburg, the Thorsbjerg piece is an ancestor of those princely animal- or bird-decorated helmets to which later literature makes frequent reference (p. 112). Tacitus notes the existence of a head-covering which he calls a *galea,* a leather or fur cap, as well as a metal helmet, the *cassis.* The corpse of the man from the Tollund bog is wearing a leather cap, but it is not the kind of protection the wearer would need against the thrust of a spear or sword.

It is remarkable that despite fairly frequent contact with Roman frontier armies, and despite endemic intertribal disputes and private feuds, no great advances were made in armour and arms, with the exception of sword-blades, during the Imperial centuries. Even as late as the sixth century, the war-gear of the Germans could be unfavourably commented upon. In some battles against late Roman armies, German weapons were primitive enough for the warriors themselves to effect repairs on them during a lull in the fighting.

Why were the Germans so ill-equipped? This inferior armament of a people devoted to fighting has usually been attributed to a scarcity of iron. This may be true for the inhabitants of some parts of free Germany, but archaeological evidence is now accumulating which shows clearly that in several regions, and particularly in Bohemia, the plentiful sources of iron-ore were being tapped and that the production of iron objects, including weapons and tools, was not universally meagre. Moreover, the quality of the forged metal is higher than has been acknowledged in the past, and in no medium is this more apparent than among the sword-blades. In north Germany, a supply of serviceable iron was freely available in the layers of bog-iron re-deposited by water action in the swamps. As forging techniques improved during the period, the use of bog-iron for large objects like weapons probably became commoner and the products more efficient. People who were short of iron could presumably obtain it by means of trade, or from subject peoples, as we hear in the case of the Celtic Cotini, whose resources of iron were a powerful attraction to their iron-hungry German neighbours.

Extreme scarcity of metal will not explain, then, Roman scorn for the poverty of German armament. Compared with the Roman army, most of the barbarian Germans *were* ill equipped, but far-reaching changes were made in the late Roman period, as skill in forging iron became more evenly distributed. Iron was not scarce. The skills needed to produce high quality tools and weapons were.

Apart from what they themselves could produce, the Germans supplemented their stocks of equipment from two main sources in succession. Before the Roman advance into western Germany, contact with La Tène cultures of the central and western Celtic lands had resulted in the importation of fine swords. Through this channel of trade and loot, the Germans probably became aware of the advantages of the two-edged sword over their own cleaver-like one-edged blades, and were persuaded to adopt the former type. From the first century BC, imports of Roman weapons, especially swords, helped many Germans to arm themselves adequately.

Rather surprisingly, great numbers of these weapons, most of them no doubt loot from successful raiding and warfare, others originally the fruits of 'gun-running' across the Roman frontiers, were not retained for earthly use, but were dedicated to the gods of war and deposited in bogs, usually after being smashed or bent. Some of the finest collections of Roman and German arms and equipment now gracing northern museums stem from the bog-deposits of Vimose, Nydam and Thorsbjerg. From the Nydam bog alone have come about 100 swords and more than 500 spear-heads, including many Roman items: enough to arm a fair-sized retinue if, as seems probable, most of this armoury was laid to rest at one time, and not deposited over many years. Unfortunately, we do not know what proportion of the captured gear was *not* offered up to the war gods, but it is likely to have been considerable, and may have made more than a little difference to the quality of German armament in some areas.

The construction of defensive earthworks is not a field in which the early Germans have enjoyed any repute. A reader of Tacitus would think that such works were beyond their powers, but recent excavations have revealed several important defended sites dating from the Roman period. Powerfully defended *oppida* on the Gallic and British model are admittedly rare, but their existence is certain. The Germans north of the Main for instance had a defended capital or stronghold on the Altenburg near Niedenstein *(Mattium)*, while pre-Roman earthworks, usually in the form of small hill-forts, exist in certain areas in Scandinavia. Moreover, defended sites were not exclusively strongholds or refuges. Several defended farms or small villages are now known in Friesland, and while these are still unmatched elsewhere in free Germany, it must be stressed that Dutch scholars have devoted a significantly greater part of their time to studying entire settlement sites than their colleagues in neighbouring countries. Certainly the German armies did not begin to rival the Romans in the construction of works connected with field-exercise, marching-camps, practice-works and permanent forts, but they were not all as inept as the words of Tacitus suggest.

The excavation of the hill-top stronghold known as the Erdenburg, near Bensberg, put the Germans in a different light as builders of defended sites. The Erdenburg is not by any means merely a refuge. It is not a remote hill-top, indeed the spur on which the fortress stands overlooks the Rhine valley from the very edge of the *Bergland*, 16 kilometres east of Cologne. Its siting thus suggests that its builders were influenced by strategic motives. The defences are sophisticated, and their builders have clearly learnt much from Celtic, if not Roman, engineers. The steep-sided, V-shaped ditches with their narrow, leg-trapping bottoms echo Roman military practice, but similar defensive ditches are also found round Celtic *oppida*. The rampart is a well-built, timber-framed structure, its foundations deeply thrust into the natural clay. In front, it is screened by two smaller timber palisades. The principal entrance was protected by a powerfully defended gatehouse, and certain sectors of the lines of rampart encircling the hill-top may have been guarded by watch towers sited at intervals.

ORGANISATION AND TACTICS

The early German armies, like the armies of the Alamanni, Franks and Lombards later, were tribes in arms, the bearing of arms being an honour shared by all adult freemen. The Germans encountered and described by Caesar elected war-chiefs who held that position for the duration of a single campaign only. A century or more later, we find two kinds of leader, the one an elected chief of the old stamp—a *dux*—and the other a *rex*, chosen from a fairly limited number of nobles. A chief of the latter type could hold his position for life, and his responsibilities may not have included leadership in war. Neither in council nor on the battlefield did any leader enjoy much authority. Once battle had been joined, his role appears to have involved little more than shouting encouragement and advice to his men, and these exhortations must normally have gone unheeded.

Very few leaders, whether *reges* or *duces,* seem to have achieved absolute authority over their forces, even for a short period of emergency. On the few occasions when such a leader did emerge, the Roman commanders generally found themselves up against it. One of Rome's most formidable opponents in the early Imperial period was Maroboduus, a chieftain of the Marcomanni, who sternly opposed the Roman movement into south Germany for some 30 years after about 9 BC. He made himself autocratic chief over this people, and instituted important changes in their organisation for war. As a result, for a short time, a German folk-unit was provided with an army which was controlled by a single, central command, and which was consequently better disciplined and more flexibly organised than was usually the case. Roman relief was great, when in AD 19 after a period of internal German dissension, Maroboduus was expelled by his countrymen and forced to seek refuge in the Roman world. In these same decades, a number of other German peoples, notably the Cherusci and the Chatti, who held the hill country east of the middle Rhine, improved their organisation and their tactics after their first brush with Rome, 'following the standards, keeping troops in reserve, and obeying commands', but little lasting impression upon barbarian warfare seems to have been made.

Tacitus leaves us in no doubt about the character of the life of the fighting men. Those who formed the retinue of a chief spent most of their time, when no fighting presented itself, in sleep and feasting, and in giving and receiving of gifts. As in most primitive and turbulent societies, the qualities which were most admired were courage and generosity. A chief gained and held his followers by gifts and hospitality, and their support enabled him to enlarge his power, his land, and the largesse at his disposal.

Tactics were of a primitive kind. A headlong initial rush in wedge-shaped formations was aimed at overpowering or intimidating their opponents. If that did not ensue, the barbarians would then try to break up the battle into a large number of single combats. Inter-German warfare might have taken place before the walls of Troy. Against disciplined infantry, such tactics had proved disastrously ineffective at Aquae Sextiae (103 BC) and at Vercellae (101 BC), but they remained the basis of German warfare until after the great migrations.

The wedge-shaped battle-units, the *cunei,* were composed of family- and kinship-groups. The Germanic term *cuneus* was used, in two senses, among Roman soldiers too. In one sense, it signified an entire regiment, presumably of Germans, such as the *cuneus* of Frisii at Housesteads on Hadrian's Wall. In the other sense, the term was translated into Roman army slang as *'caput porcinum'* or swine's head, indicating that the German manner of ordering the battle-line in wedges had penetrated the Roman system to some extent, obviously through the agency of German auxiliary troops. Precisely what a swine's head had to do with a battle-unit is not quite clear, but the explanation may lie in the protective powers believed to have been exercised by the boar-image over the German fighting man (p. 112). The *cuneus* might be preceded into battle by 'images and standards taken down from sacred groves'. The images are likely to have been figures of gods, and the standards too may have been quasi-religious in character. The boar is a prominent standard-emblem among the Germans. It appears, for instance, on the German standards which are shown on the sarcophagus of a Roman general A. Julius Pompilius, who commanded an army against the Marcomanni in the late second century.

At their most effective, German tactics were those of the guerrilla. Against Roman armies of the early Empire, a favourite manoeuvre was to nag the flanks of an army crossing a clearing by making short rushes from the shelter of the forest, and retiring before the Roman infantry had time to come to grips. If the legionaries did make contact with the German forces, the issue was rarely in doubt for long. The barbarian rushes might try the patience, but hardly the skill, of trained soldiers.

## GERMANS IN THE ROMAN ARMY

The Romans were always prepared to erect a screen of protection beyond the frontiers by entering into treaties with barbarian leaders. These agreements were principally designed to prevent those same barbarians from plundering the frontier districts, but they also produced barbarian forces who might be employed on tasks of frontier defence, either near their native soil or in distant provinces. These *foederati* seem to have performed useful service to the Roman state for as long as they were used in limited numbers and provided that those barbarians employed on occasional campaigns within the Empire returned to their own lands when the campaign was over.

After AD 376, there came a significant change. The Visigoths were granted land in the Balkans at this time, in return for military service on Rome's behalf. Other federate groups, including Burgundi and Alani, lodged themselves on the northern frontiers and achieved recognition on similar terms. Well before the opening of the fifth century, the barbarisation of the frontier armies was well advanced. These federates had more profit from the arrangement than their employers, opportunity usually being found to enlarge their easily won lands. The barbarians recruited into the regular army units, however, gave the Romans much better value for money. Relatively few deserted or betrayed their masters, and the great gaps torn in the Roman ranks by disastrous battles like that at Adrianople were adequately filled by these recruits.

The most striking characteristic of German warfare throughout the four centuries in which contact was maintained with the Roman Empire is its conservatism in the face of good reason for change. Neither in tactics, nor in the body-armour of the common soldiers were any permanent improvements wrought. In the quality of the weapons, notably the swords, there was some advance, as we have seen, but the mass of the soldiery derived little benefit from it. This stagnation in military affairs can only be explained by the German attitude to war. Above all, their view of war seems to have been sporting, in some aspects almost gentlemanly, and the warfare of the time was waged with the spirit and devotion of professionals, but with tactics which did not rise above the amateur.

## THE PERIOD OF MIGRATION

The military organisation of the Germanic tribes shows hardly any development from the time of their first great successes against the late Roman frontier armies until long after their settlement in the old frontier provinces. A late sixth-century writer might as well be describing the Germans of the early Roman period when he records that 'the Franks, Lombards and their like are adherents of single combat, on horseback or on foot. Should they find themselves in a confined space, the horsemen, if there are any among them, dismount and fight on foot.' Since they fought in family groups and not in ordered formations (see above p. 106), 'if it happens that their friends fall, they expose themselves to danger to avenge them. . . . They do not obey their leaders. Headstrong, despising strategy, caution or foresight, they scorn every tactical order, especially the cavalry.'

Despite the relatively frequent references by late Roman and Byzantine writers to barbarian cavalry, few, if any, German peoples seem to have relied principally upon cavalry before the sixth century at the earliest. The Frankish armies carried through their first great conquests as predominantly infantry forces. The first mention of the cavalry arm comes in connection with the Frankish invasion of Italy in AD 539, but later references, illustrating the limited uses to which mounted troops were put, make it clear that progress in this department of war was slow. The Alamanni, the Vandals and the Visigoths made use of mounted men, but most of these were probably nobles. Gothic cavalry, it is true, played an important role in the shattering defeat of the Romans at Adrianople in AD 378, but that great achievement is to be chiefly credited to the performance of the barbarian infantry. The common soldiers of the early Anglo-Saxon peoples in Britain employed cavalry in no greater numbers than the Franks, but mentions of war-horses in Beowulf echo references in Anglo-Saxon laws and make it clear that the charger and his trappings could form part of the aristocratic warrior's equipment.

'The protector of nobles bade eight horses with gold-plated bridles be brought into the hall within the building. On one of them was placed a saddle cunningly inlaid, adorned with jewels—that was the war-seat of the mighty king when Healfdene's son wished to take part in the play of swords.'

## ARMOUR

Throughout the Migration period, as earlier, protection of the body does not seem to have been enjoyed by the rank and file, except when they were fortunate enough to take it from a fallen foe. Chiefs and *Heerkönige* alone had the means to command such protective gear as a matter of course, and it is from the graves of such men that we are most fully informed about the full German panoply. Of the Franks who suffered defeat at the hands of Narses, only a few had armour or helmets. The common foot-soldiers fought naked to the waist, their lower limbs being covered by breeches of linen or leather. Occasionally their legs were bound with puttees formed of strips of leather or coarse cloth. In equipment, and in tactical skill, these Franks were no better off than the Germans who had faced the armies of Caesar and Augustus six centuries or more earlier.

Frankish laws estimate a helmet as equivalent to a horse, a good mail-coat as equal to two horses or six oxen. This high valuation is echoed by the comparative rarity of helmets and other body-coverings in the archaeological record of all regions of barbarian Europe. Even princely graves may contain nothing more of armour than a helmet and a shield. A description of a sixth-century Frankish count of Tours, Leudast, from the pen of Gregory of Tours catalogues the principal pieces of armour worn by a noble. Leudast's body was covered by a coat or corselet of mail, probably the simple ring-mail evidenced by several finds. A gorget protected the throat, a helmet the head. A spear was held ready in one hand, and a quiver hung from a

*53 The chieftain's helmet from Morken (near Euskirchen, Germany), about AD 600*

baldric. We may presume the presence of a bow to serve him if he survived the ambush, which Leudast, with good reason, daily expected.

The helmet was a piece of war-gear fit for a noble or a king, and thus was frequently celebrated in the literature of the time. The magnificent helmet from the grave of a Frankish chief at Morken in the Rhineland illustrates in detail an aristocratic helmet of about AD 600. This is a representative of the *Spangenhelm* type. In shape, the cap is conical, its main characteristic being the fact that it is built up of leaf-shaped segments of iron attached to an iron framework. This framework is a horizontal headband and a number of vertical bands converging at the apex of the cap. Hinged cheek-pieces and a rivetted noseguard, broken off in the Morken piece, add protection to the face. The neck was shielded by a guard of iron ring-mail hanging from the rear of the headband. The iron plates covering the skull were coated externally with gilded bronze and a leather lining was also provided. This was no mere parade- or prestige-helmet. The gilding has been worn away in patches and deep sword-dents are visible in the cap.

The Morken helmet, in common with many others from rich warrior-graves distributed over the enormous tract of country from Bohemia to the English Channel, and from Scandinavia to the Balkans, is fairly certainly an import from north Italy. The ultimate derivation is probably from a near-Asian, perhaps Iranian, source. This Asian helmet-form was freely imitated in Ostrogothic and in Byzantine workshops, and thence numbers were distributed among the barbarians of central and northern Europe. Some of the soldiers in fifth-century Byzantine armies wore them, but most of the surviving specimens have come from barbarian graves.

The *Spangenhelm* was not the only type in use. Several helmets were found in the richly furnished graves at Vendel and Valsgärde (Sweden), some of them sufficiently well pre-served for a reconstruction to be attempted. One from Vals-gärde has a complex mesh of cruciform and Y-shaped pieces of iron filling up the spaces between the iron bands of the frame-work. Protection may have been given to the neck and cheeks by an encircling curtain of mail, and in front an iron nose-guard completes the armour of the piece.

Since the helmet was part of the insignia of a chief as much as a piece of armour, we would expect to find some examples which are more decorative than protective. A boy-prince buried in a Frankish church beneath Cologne Cathedral had in his grave a *Spangenhelm,* the cap of which was composed of 12 horn segments, originally attached to bronze ribs (below, p. 156). Descriptions of helmets in Old Norse and Anglo-Saxon literature commonly mentioned boar-images as surmounting or otherwise decorating them: 'The fear was less by just so much as woman's strength, a woman's war-terror, is as compared with that of a man, when the ornamented, hammer-forged blade, the blood-stained sword trusty of edge, cleaves through the boar-image on the helmet of the foe.' Another passage from *Beowulf* indicates that the boar-image had apotropaic power over the wearer and his followers: 'Above the cheek-guards shone the boar-image, covered with gold, gleaming and tempered. The fierce-hearted boar held guard over the warlike men.' Other helmets were surmounted by bird-images, including those of the raven, while the raven, the wolf and the eagle—all associated with the grimmer aspects of the carnage of battle—are frequently met with in poetry, and on actual helmets, shield-mounts and weapons. One from Vendel, with a bird crowning the crest reminds us that at this time, Sweden, north Germany and England shared in the same cultural and artistic *milieu*.

WEAPONS AND TACTICS
*The Franks*
Frankish tactical methods were of the simplest, as Agathias, a sixth-century Byzantine writer, reveals:

> They have hardly any horsemen, but their foot-soldiery are bold and well-practised in war. They bear swords and shields, but never use the sling or bow. Their missiles are axes and barbed javelins *(angones)*. These last are not very long, and can be used either to throw or to stab. The iron of the head runs so far down the shaft that very little of the wood remains unprotected. In battle they hurl these javelins, and if they strike an enemy, the barbs are so firmly fixed in his body that he cannot draw the weapon out. If it strikes a shield, it is impossible for him to get rid of it by cutting off the head for the iron runs too far down the shaft. At this moment the Frank rushes in, places his foot on the butt as it trails on the ground, and pulling the shield down, cleaves his unprotected foe through the head, or pierces his breast with a second spear.

The most distinctively Frankish weapons in this account of Agathias are the barbed javelin *(ango)* and the throwing-axe *(franciska)*. Both were also employed by the Alamanni, but it was the Franks who developed their use most fully. The *ango* is clearly a descendant, however remote, of the Roman *pilum*, the throwing-weapon of the legionaries, designed for discharge at an enemy thirty yards away. The *franciska* was in use among the Alamanni during the fourth century, but has no history before then, axes being rarely used on the battlefield. It was a single-bladed instrument with a carefully weighted head, curved on its outer face and deeply hollowed within. Its skilful use, being hurled just before closing with the enemy, earned considerable respect for the Frankish infantryman, and for two centuries it remained the national weapon. The great Frankish victory over the Visigoths at Vouillé in AD 507 was a victory of throwing-weapons over lances.

After about AD 600, as dated grave-finds show, the weapons of the Franks underwent a considerable change. The *franciska* and the two-edged long sword or *spatha* were replaced by the short, single-edged sword, the sax. This was a versatile weapon, some 18 inches in length, which might be used to thrust, stab, or even to throw. The shield was usually broad and oval, or rectangular, and was equipped with the customary iron boss and rim-binding.

*54, 55 Frankish* ango *from Krefeld-Gellep (Germany) and* ango *from Perchtoldsdorf (near Vienna)*

*56* Franciska *from Krefeld-Gellep*

## The Anglo-Saxons

Closest of all the Teutonic peoples to the Franks in weapons and tactics were the Anglo-Saxon settlers in southern England. It has already been noted that, like the Franks and the rest, their use of cavalry was negligible. The offensive weapon of the rank and file was the spear, of which several types are documented, that with a long leaf- or lozenge-shaped head being the best known. These spear-heads commonly measure between 10 inches and 18 inches in length. The *sax* was frequently carried by the fifth- and sixth-century warrior, in Anglo-Saxon England as well as in Frankish Gaul, and was closely, almost mystically, associated with the Saxon name and race. The earlier Anglo-Saxon swords are rather broad, two to three feet long, two-edged and pointed. Body-armour is ill-attested, except for the leading warriors. Helmets are even more rarely mentioned in Anglo-Saxon law than in Frankish, and only three specimens have been recorded—all from princely graves. Leather caps may have protected lesser heads, but probably not many. The shield might be oval or rectangular. Late Saxon manuscripts show some shields as convex, and a few actual specimens from the pagan centuries were similarly formed. The finest examples come from the regal cenotaph of Sutton Hoo and from a grave in the Petersfinger (Wilts.) cemetery.

## The Lombards

The war-gear of the Lombards is better documented in the Danube valley, their home from the later fifth century, than in their ultimate north Italian domicile. Again, the lance was the weapon of the common warrior. Two main types can be distinguished, one with a broad head for stabbing, the other with a narrow point well-suited to throwing. A rarer, longer type also designed for throwing, illustrated by the example from Perchtoldsdorf near Vienna, is reminiscent of the Frankish *ango*. Another tenuous link with the Frankish west is the occasional occurrence of the throwing-axe. Even at a comparatively early date, the Lombards put more trust in cavalry than most of their neighbours, and Byzantine writers have many stories demonstrating the power and skill of their mounted forces. These were led by well-armoured knights, some of whom wore mail-shirts, helmets and greaves. The weapons of these horsemen were the long *spatha* and the lance. Some of the latter were evidently very long. One mounted Lombard champion speared a Byzantine soldier and lifted his catch high in the air on the lance-end. Contemporary historians and the Lombard law-codes, with their frequent mention of horses, horse-breeding and horse-stealing, show this people as more commonly aware of the power and usefulness of the horse. As revealing a sidelight on this aspect of their life is the occurrence in a number of warrior-graves in north Italy of the skeletons of horses and of horse trappings.

From Lombard territory have come a number of richly decorated shields. These were normally round wooden boards with several metal mounts arranged round the edge. These are products of seventh-century workshops, but perhaps are late representatives of a tradition which began in the Migration Period. Examples from Stabio (Tessin) and Lucca bear symbols which are probably Christian: a warrior, presumably Christ, who holds a standard which is surmounted by a dove; a chalice. Another, found at Münzesheim (Baden) and evidently an import from Lombard territory, bears a number of crosses on its boss.

## THE SWORD

Of all weapons used by Germanic peoples, we know most about the sword, a weapon which, in northern Europe at any rate, was wielded by the richer warriors only. The sword was more than a weapon to the Germanic mind. It was closely associated with many significant aspects of human affairs: above all, the duties of the king, the fealty of a warrior to his leader, the swearing of solemn vows, the achieving of manhood, the rites of the funeral. The sword was the 'shoulder-companion' of the king and the warrior, his 'comrade'. Without his sword, a man was a cipher, unable to protect himself and his own. A tenth-century swordsman could affirm that he was as good as dead without his sword. 'The trolls may have my life indeed, when I can no more redden keen Laufi.' Small wonder that an aura of mystery and a canopy of lore hangs about the sword, its deeds and its making.

Some of the finest blades of the Migration and Viking periods have long been known to display striking zig-zag,

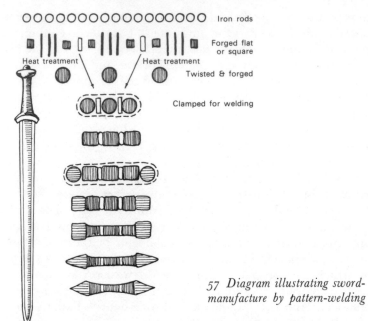

Iron rods

Forged flat or square

Heat treatment

Heat treatment

Twisted & forged

Clamped for welding

*57 Diagram illustrating sword-manufacture by pattern-welding*

herringbone and wavy patterns in the component metal. These patterns, a product of the forging process, seem to have penetrated deeply into the thoughts of those who saw and handled such weapons. Sword-names like 'fish-back' and 'Veigarr'—descriptive of a richly brocaded fabric—surely refer to pattern-welded blades. 'Rain-patterned' swords of the sagas, and a blade along which creeps a serpent, are similarly inspired. The process by which these blades were made has been carefully studied and reproduced by modern scholars. Three bundles of wrought-iron rods and strips, together with two 'filler' rods, were forged and then twisted into a single rod. This was to form the centre of the blade. Two smaller rods produced in the same way were then clamped to either side of the first. These were to be the cutting edges. The whole was then lightly forged. The centre of the blade was shaped with the chisel and the cutting edges received their final forging. The complicated patterns produced by the structure of the twist-welded rods could then be brought out by filing, etching and polishing.

This process had already produced fine swords for the

northern Germans in the fourth and fifth centuries, and Roman military workshops of the second and third centuries had been familiar with the technique. Whether the Roman army smiths were responsible for its invention, or whether Celtic smiths brought it into the service of Rome is still undecided. Nor are we better informed about the siting of the pattern-welding workshops which supplied the migrating peoples. The Rhineland and the old Roman province of Noricum on the Upper Danube are two strong candidates.

A number of swords have a ring attached to the hilt, and occasionally a second, loose, ring is linked with this. The significance of these ring-swords, and the area in which they originated, has been much debated. Several have been found in south-eastern Britain and since some of these are at least as early as any from Frankish Gaul or Scandinavia, the ringed hilt may have a Kentish origin. The rings clearly have had no utilitarian purpose, and it is almost certain that they fulfilled a ritual or symbolic function, possibly symbolising the 'sword-alliance' between two warriors, one of whom had presented the

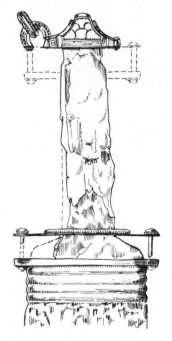

*58 Ring-sword from Faver-sham (Kent)*

sword to the other, or the allegiance of a warrior to his king, the giver of swords. Other attachments, either to hilt or scabbard, are evidenced by grave-finds, and the special nature of several of these—balls or beads of amber, crystal or even of meerschaum, and small pyramids of richly ornamented metal, indicates some magical or ritual intention.

It is clear from heroic poetry that individual swords might be so highly prized that they were handed on from father to son. Some might be of considerable antiquity before being laid to rest in a warrior's grave. Most of these long-lived swords derived their powers from their association with some famed warrior or king. Others were revered as distinguished weapons chiefly because of their great age and the durability implied by the very fact of their survival. The walls of the Germanic hall, however, were no museum of handsome antique weapons which were never used.

Scabbards were normally constructed of wood, or wood and leather, and thus only any metal fittings they might have had are commonly found. Some of the finer scabbards, as well as the sword-hilts and pommels, were decorated with nielloed or otherwise inlaid mounts, and lined with fur or felt. The garb of the well-turned-out warrior was completed by a belt round the waist, from which his sword and dagger could hang. Among the Alamanni, at least, the sword might be carried in one of two ways, either hanging from the waist belt or slung from a shoulder strap.

THE BOW

The bow and arrow, exotic in Merovingian Gaul and Anglo-Saxon England, was more widely used by other Germans. The Alamanni used a simple D-shaped one-piece bow, and, very rarely, a bow composed of several different materials. Bone or horn was usually combined with wood in these composite bows.

In the late Roman period the long-bow put in an appearance in the north. From which part of Europe this weapon was introduced is unknown but it was not from either the Roman Empire or from the nomadic peoples. Probably this was something the Germans developed for themselves. The fact that about 40 long-bows and several bundles of arrows were present in the Nydam deposit suggests that small units of bowmen may have been used in the later fourth century specifically against armoured Roman troops. Some of the Nydam arrowheads are narrow and heavy, and thus well suited to piercing body-armour.

With the gradual development of cavalry power in several parts of Western Europe, greater use of the bow, well adapted to use by mounted troops, might have been made. A few princely graves of the third century and later contain silver and bronze arrow-heads, but it is hard to establish how far the process of developing the *Fernkampf* went among the Germans before the ninth century. Among two important peoples, however, before the sixth century, infantrymen with bows were well established. The main body of the Visigothic armies were bow- and spear-bearing infantrymen. Most of the mounted men were chiefs and their retainers, wielding long, two-edged swords which they had derived from the weapons of the Sarmatian inhabitants of the Pontic region. After the Visigothic settlement of Spain, our knowledge of their warfare is scanty, not least because it was not a wide-spread custom among them to provide weapons as grave-furniture for the dead warrior.

Archer-infantrymen also formed a substantial element of the armies of the Ostrogoths by the sixth century. Fortunately for us, their siege of Rome in 537–8 was described by Procopius, who was especially interested in weapons. One of his passages reveals in lucid detail how the inflexibility of barbarian tactics could lead them to a downfall. The opposing Romans and allied Huns were mainly mounted archers, who found that it was easy to pick off the Ostrogothic cavalry, armed with swords and spears, at long range, and at the same time to prevent their foot archers to advance into a good firing position. The formidable combination of the horse and the bow was coming into its own at last. Although the Ostrogoths and the Vandals developed the cavalry arm more rapidly than the other barbarians, their contact with the formidably accurate Hunnic mounted archers in Central Europe did not teach them quickly enough the full potential of cavalry power, particularly when allied with the bow.

SIEGE-WARFARE

In assessing the early Germanic peoples as exponents of siege-warfare, we are at a great disadvantage. All the surviving literature is, of course, written from the Roman side. If we believed all it records about the incompetence of the Germans as tacticians and as stormers of cities, we could well ask why it was the barbarians eventually won the struggle. Ridicule of one's opponents in war, his peacetime customs as well as his way of conducting his campaigns, is a remarkably successful way of maintaining morale, and we should therefore approach the surviving accounts of German siege-warfare with some reserve. They did after all overturn powerfully defended frontiers and shatter an urban civilisation. Not many of the German successes are recorded, and none are told in detail. Certainly there were many failures, and unfortunately for German repute in later times, several of these are easily made ridiculous.

The earlier invaders of the Mediterranean provinces can have found the siege of a city ill-suited to their temperament or their purposes. Fritigern of the Visigoths 'had made his peace with walls'. Plundering bands will have given walled settlements a wide berth, and devoted more of their attention to unprotected villas and villages. But towns with walls were worth plundering if the defences could be forced, and the attempt was often made. The attackers were at a disadvantage on two main counts. First, few of them ever seem to have developed the art of making siege-engines, whether artillery like the Roman *balistae,* for throwing stones and bolts, or towers, mounds and mantlets to act as platforms for assault on the walls. Some moves in this direction were made, but the Romans always professed to be unmoved by these barbarian enterprises. Witigis and his Ostrogoths in their siege of Rome in 536 brought up four great battering-rams on wheels, so heavy that 50 men were needed to bring them into operation. Wheeled towers of timber were built to equal the height of the city wall, and were drawn forward by oxen. But the Roman archers scotched the plan by shooting down the beasts, leaving the towers stranded some way from the defences. Witigis persisted with his engine-building, only to have the results set on fire by the defenders.

Secondly, an organised commissariat seems hardly to have existed before the eighth century. The slow decay of the Roman road-system behind the frontiers, and the piecemeal character of barbarian campaigns, meant that the provision of supplies for the armies was haphazard and frequently broke down altogether. Most German hosts made no provision for supplies before the campaign began, so that the movement of an army might be determined, in large measure, by the availability of food on its route. Inevitably, the size of armies too was limited by foodstocks in the districts through which they hope to pass, and in consequence one effective Roman defensive ploy was to stockpile as much food as possible out of German reach within defended forts, posting-stations and towns. This barbarian incapacity to support armies for a long period was a source of comfort to Roman and Byzantine city populations. Safe behind their walls they could confidently await the eventual withdrawal of a hungry, and very occasionally a gorged invader. When food and plunder were not available, armies melted away. This fact, and chronic indiscipline, meant that campaigns with long-term objectives could rarely be carried out.

A major invasion of Italy by an army of Goths led by Radagaisus in AD 405 came to an ignominious end among the barren Tuscan hills for this very reason. The comfortably supplied Roman forces and their barbarian auxiliaries, 'eating, drinking, playing' according to Orosius, who describes the incident, locked up the starving intruders against the encircling hills in the neighbourhood of Faesulae. Radagaisus despaired of his enterprise and made a bolt for freedom, only to fall into Roman hands. His ravenous and demoralised followers were sold off as slaves, but shortly died off in such numbers that their buyers saw no return for their money. Late in 377, an army of Goths were placed rather like that army of Radagaisus, hemmed in among the bewildering gullies on the slopes of Mount Haemus in Thrace, and they would have suffered the same fate as Radagaisus' men had not a few messengers slipped out and raised aid from a wandering band of Huns and Alans.

THE SIZE OF ARMIES

It follows therefore that the normal Germanic raiding party or campaigning army was very small. Armies of several thousands would have joined battle only in the course of a mass-migration or in defence of the territory of a tribe against an invader. A chapter in the late seventh-century law-code of Ine of Wessex is instructive: 'We use the term "thieves" if the number of men does not exceed seven, "band of marauders" for a number between seven and 35; anything beyond this is a *here*.'

*Here* may be translated either as 'raid' or 'army'. The supposed 10,000 Alamanni who raided Gaul in the 360s represent a pardonable exaggeration. Several companies of Franks encountered by the emperor Julian in Gaul together totalled 600 warriors and were considered substantial opposition. The three shiploads of Angles whom Vortigern invited into Britain, according to one version of the Anglo-Saxon Chronicle, the same number of ships that came with Aelle, or the five that came with Cerdic, may belong to saga rather than to history, but it is usually overlooked that the first figure is found already in Gildas and it may well be close to the truth. The Alamannic army that crossed the Alps in 457 and was destroyed in the Bellinzona region is said to have numbered 900 men. The Visigothic warriors who fought at Adrianople were perhaps counted in their thousands. The unusually precise figures of Ostrogothic garrisons in Italy given by Procopius in his account of the Imperial reconquest in the second quarter of the sixth century take us nearer the truth than the supposedly many tens of thousands defeated by much smaller Imperial forces in a single battle. They vary from two instances of 4,000 in 538 and 540 respectively, to several examples of only 400–500. On the basis of these and other figures, it has been calculated that the total of Ostrogothic warriors at the beginning of these wars was something over 30,000, but several thousands less than this in the last phase. And it is beyond dispute that except perhaps in the final battles nothing remotely near this total was ever assembled in one place.

FURTHER READING

The classic work of M. Jahn, *Die Bewaffnung der Germanen in der älteren Eisenzeit* is out of date but still a valuable collection of material. The literary sources are treated by E. A. Thompson, *The Early Germans,* Chap. 4. H. R. Ellis Davidson, *The Sword in Anglo-Saxon England* (Oxford) is of much wider importance than its title suggests.

# 6

# Religious life

Sources for early German religious beliefs may be said to go back to the Bronze Age, for the prehistory of the subject is documented by the rock-pictures of Scandinavia. The mythological and religious scenes represented there can, many of them, be interpreted in the light of what is known of later German beliefs and practices, but at their most illuminating they leave much unexplained. Most of the rock-pictures date from the middle and late Bronze Age, especially from about 1000–750 BC, but a number appear to belong to the Iron Age and the Roman period. For the last-named period, Roman writers again come to our aid, and some of what they have to say is corroborated by archaeological evidence. In discussing what Tacitus and the others have to say about German cults, it will be as well to bear in mind that the German tribes covered immense tracts of land and that the circumstances of isolation in which most communities must have passed their existence were conducive to the development of regional and even local differences. Ancient writers were not always aware of these.

The religious beliefs of the later pagan period are a considerable subject on their own, so great is the body of evidence provided by the sagas and by the great compilation of the old German myths by a thirteenth-century Icelandic scholar of outstanding gifts, Snorri Sturluson. There has been debate as to how accurate a picture of Germanic paganism he gives, since he was writing two centuries after the north became Christian, but his general account of mythology is to be trusted. In this aspect of early German life, it is possible to discern certain threads which run through the Iron Age, the Roman period and on into the hey-day of the Vikings. It is difficult, if not pointless, to cut those threads at any point and therefore the successors of the early northern gods are given their place in the following pages.

### THE WAR-GODS

German cults of the warrior-god are very closely connected with those of the Celtic lands, illustrating once more the strong cultural ties between northern and central Europe, especially among the leading elements in society. For it was among chiefs and warriors that the gods of battle would find most honour. The dead warriors feasting in the hall of the warrior-god is perhaps the most widely known concept of early German religion, but even this concept may have reached northern Europe through contact with Celtic leaders. The earliest German war-gods and their worship are shown to us most reliably by Roman writers. They were deeply impressed, and appalled, by the bloodthirsty rites of some German peoples, and by any standards their accounts rank as tales of horror. Archaeological finds add some support, however, to what Strabo, Tacitus, Procopius and Jordanes have to say, and their descriptions must be treated with respect.

What appalled the Romans most of all was that human sacrifices were offered to the war-god. This aspect of the cult can be traced throughout the entire pagan period. Strabo describes how white-clad priestesses of the Cimbri sacrificed selected prisoners of war by hanging them up over large bronze bowls and slitting their throats, so that their blood flowed down into the vessels beneath. Another writer, Orosius, tells of the fate of prisoners and booty taken by the same people in 105 BC

> Following a strange and unusual vow, they began to destroy all that they had taken. Clothing was cut to pieces and thrown away. Gold and silver was thrown into the river, the breastplates of men were cut to pieces, horsegear smashed and the beasts themselves drowned in whirlpools. The men were hanged from trees, with nooses round their necks.

Sacrifice by hanging recurs again and again in our sources, both during the Imperial period and in the latest pagan centuries. The dedication to the god of the weapons of a foe, and the body of the foe himself, if victory was granted to the suppliant, is another recurring motif. When the Hermunduri and Chatti disputed possession of a stretch of river which ran between their territories, each side vowed to sacrifice the foe and his equipment to the war-gods (termed Mars and Mercury by Tacitus, who describes the event) if victory were granted to them. The Hermunduri won, and performed what they had vowed to do.

Archaeological finds dramatically support these passages from classical writers by producing the remains of sacrificial rites of this kind. The peat-bogs of Denmark and Schleswig-Holstein in particular bear witness to the influence exerted on the German mind by the power of the gods of war. The great deposits of war-booty in the bogs and pools of Nydam, Thorsbjerg, Kragehul and Vimose were excavated long ago and thus details of how the masses of equipment had accumulated may have eluded their investigators. But it is certain that the Thorsbjerg bog was the scene of numerous ceremonies over a lengthy period, whereas elsewhere, for instance at Nydam, the deposits of shattered arms probably belong to one great occasion. In the case of the most recently examined of these sites, Ejsbol, there seem to have been two major depositions of arms within a relatively short time. The largest of these votive deposits date from the late Roman period, a time when the military initiative was decidedly with the barbarian powers, and when the gods of war were very much to the fore.

The name of the greatest early German war-god was Tiwaz, or Tiw, called Tyr by Snorri and other later writers. He was a sky-god as well as the lord of battle and the name Tiwaz may be philologically connected with Zeus, the Greek god of heaven. He was also concerned with the life of the community, as the guardian of law and order, and in one Roman guise he appears as Mars Thingsus, the god who presides over or protects the *Thing* or assembly. Probably the earlier bog-deposits were designed to appease Tiwaz, but otherwise we have very little indication of how he was worshipped. The Semnones of the regions between the Oder and the Elbe, worshipped their supreme deity in a very peculiar rite, and one feature suggests that he might have been Tiwaz. Yearly the Semnones assembled in a sacred wood, where they witnessed a human sacrifice. After they had entered the wood they were bound, by this act doing obeisance to the god, and if any fell to the ground during the ceremonies, they may not struggle to their feet but had to roll along the ground. This odd procedure recalls the power of Tiwaz, and later Odin, recorded in other sources, to bind his devotees.

It is not known when Tiwaz, or any of the other war-gods, began to be worshipped in northern Europe. Nor do we know when he began to be supplanted as the supreme war-deity by Wodan, but the process probably had started well before about AD 400. Wodan was normally equated with Mercury by Roman writers, and this at first sight seems strange. The identification with Mercury, however, was reasonable. Not until late in the Roman period did Wodan emerge as a great god of war, for war was not his only concern. He had strong connexions with the chthonic powers as the guide of souls to the underworld, with the trading activities of mankind, and with intellectual learning. These three distinct spheres of interest were in the Roman world presided over by Mercury. In the myths current towards the end of the heathen period especially in Viking Scandinavia, Wodan's prestige is overshadowed by that of his son, Odin, the ruler-patriarch of Asgard, realm of the gods.

The character of Odin is complex in the extreme. He was descended on one side from giants and on the other from Buri, son of the primeval cow. He was possessed of great wisdom, especially of wisdom normally hidden from men, and was familiar with the working of magic. The creation of men, and probably of other living creatures, lay within his power, and to men he gave the arts of runes and of poetry. Above all, Odin was a god of war and strife, the lord of battles and of the battle-slain. Few gods were so frequently pictured in human guise. Odin was old, as befitted the chief god and father of mankind, one-eyed, grey-bearded and tall. Often he wore a broad hat. Despite his gifts of poetry and writing to men, Odin's aspect is always grim and sinister. His magic could strike panic terror into his enemies and make their weapons useless. His own warriors could be inspired with a mystic rage, the rage of the *berserks,* which made them fight with the ferocity and strength of wild animals, but his protection did not extend over all those who served him. Strife between kinsmen was his especial delight. Odin was the arch-deceiver, as well as the lord of battle. In him men saw the horror and futility of war, and nothing of the nobility and courage of the ideal soldier.

Besides Tiwaz and Wodan, a third war-god was honoured by the German peoples, Donar, Thor or Thunar. He was considered by many north Germans of the later pagan centuries the most noble and powerful of all the gods, and his influence seems to have greatly increased after the end of the period of migration. Originally, Thunar was a god of natural forces, and his constant companion, the hammer Mjöllnir, symbolised thunder, the most violent activity of the elements. His association with the weather was, however, overlaid by many other responsibilities. Thunar was a manly warrior, a traveller, a glutton, but a great thinker also, a cunning god who could change his shape to achieve his ends. In some respects, he recalls the Greek Herakles, but resemblances with the Indian god Indra are even closer, leading scholars to conclude that Indra and Thunar are descended from the same Indo-European ancestor.

The early history of his cult is obscure. Tacitus mentions that the Germans of the first century AD worshipped a god (whom he calls Hercules) who might be lauded as the strongest of men by warriors advancing into battle. This sounds like Thunar, and one or two epithets attributed to Hercules on Roman inscriptions in the Rhine valley, for example Hercules Magasanus on the lower Rhine and Hercules Saxsanus in several stone quarries on the middle Rhine, hint at local German cults of a deity who resembled Hercules in his strength and endurance. By medieval writers, however, Thunar was normally equated with Jupiter, the god of sky and thunder, an association which is more appropriate to the German god's original *milieu*.

## THE GODS OF FERTILITY

Fertility cults naturally had considerable influence among the lower levels of German society, and there is every indication that the life-giving forces held not merely the peasants in their power. As is to be expected, fertility symbols of many kinds appear in the Bronze Age rock pictures of Scandinavia, but of course no details of the cults are made known to us until the Roman period. In the first century AD, we hear from Tacitus, the seven tribes inhabiting the Danish peninsula and Schleswig-

*59 Wooden ornament representing cow's horns, from Ferwerd (Friesland). Probably a symbol of fertility*

Holstein worshipped a female deity called Nerthus, and the Roman author likened her to the Earth-Mother. She could intervene in the affairs of men, and occasionally—probably annually—she visited her worshippers in a wagon, bringing fertility to men and crops. But she, or her image, was never visible to her devotees, and none but her priest might look inside her holy cart or even touch it. He alone could sense the presence of the god. This and certain other mysterious elements in her cult recalls Near Eastern and Graeco-Roman fertility worship. During her visits to the world of men, warfare was forbidden and iron objects were hidden away. Between her progresses among her people, Nerthus and her wagon were restored to a sacred grove on an island, and each excursion was followed by ritual washing in a lake of the image or symbol of the goddess, the wagon and its awning. The slaves who performed this task were drowned after discharging their duty.

Two richly ornamented ceremonial carts from a bog at Dejbjerg (Jutland) have often been associated by archaeologists with cult-progresses like those described by Tacitus, and the coincidence of their find-spot with the area indicated by Tacitus as the centre of the cult of Nerthus is clearly too striking to be ignored. These beautifully made carts were produced by Celtic craftsmen, quite probably in Gaul, in the century before Christ. They were found, dismantled, in a peat-bog, suggesting that they had finally been offered to the deity whom they had served.

Another deity drawn in a wagon is encountered far to the south-east of Denmark. During a persecution of Christians among the Goths in the late fourth century AD, the Gothic leader Athanaric commanded that an idol of some unknown kind (it is simply called *xoanon* by the Greek writer who records the affair) be placed on a wagon and drawn round to all those suspected of being Christians, they being ordered to make sacrifices to it. Although we are not told what kind of deity the *xoanon* represented, the wheeling about of the image on a cart recalls the fructifying of fields and stock which was also the concern of Nerthus.

In the Migration period, and later, another fertility deity, a male god, travelled round the lands of his people at the time of harvest, bringing prosperity and peace with him. This god was Freyr, the son of Njord, whose name suggests a link with Nerthus. Snorri tells us that Freyr and his Freyja belonged to a group of divine spirits known as the Vanir, whose general sphere of interest was the well-being and fertility of men and their world. Some aspects of the worship of Freyr are almost identical with what is known of the cult of Nerthus. No weapons might be taken into his temples, and blood shed on land sacred to Freyr roused the anger of the god. One of the sagas mentions an especially fertile field, which appears to have belonged to a neighbouring temple of Freyr, and certain Norwegian place-names and field-names incorporating his own may mark sites of his worship. Appropriately, marriage and the creation of children also came within his power.

The sources for the later pagan period make it clear that Freyr was the outstanding fertility deity in northern Europe at that time, but there is no clear knowledge of the process by which he emerged into that pre-eminent position. In the Roman and migration periods, both male and female deities of fructification were worshipped. Some scholars have seen Njord-Nerthus as such a pair, with Njord, and later his son Freyr, becoming the dominant partner, but a conclusion has not yet been reached on the point. Of one thing there is no doubt. In the Migration period and later, no female deity, not even Fryja, challenged Freyr's position.

The horse and the boar were closely associated with Freyr and Freyja. Sacred horses were kept in or near Freyr's holy places in Norway and Iceland, some of them being destined to provide food for the god, others probably being kept to show their paces in horse-races at his festivals. The boar was closely connected with fertility, and with chthonic cults, in many early European cultures, and in early Germany it combined the duties of a fertility image with those of a standard which protected the warrior (p.112).

Another symbol which links Freyr with both fertility and funerary rites is the ship. The ship symbol occurs among the Bronze Age carvings, and like the wagon of Nerthus was later used to convey the god of plenty about the countryside at certain seasons. Ship-processions in several parts of Scandinavia survived the strictures of mediaeval clerics and remained the basis for rituals of field-blessing until relatively recent times.

RELIGIOUS SCULPTURE

If one of Tacitus' statements were taken as literal truth, we would not expect to find religious sculpture at all in northern Europe. According to the Roman historian, the Germans did not think it consonant with divinity to make anthropomorphic figures or statues of their gods. Of stone reliefs at this time, it is true, there is hardly a trace, but simple wooden figure-sculpture made good the deficiency to some extent. All the surviving examples of these wooden figures come from peat-bogs, and in all cases either their inherent character or their immediate surroundings mark them out as adjuncts of religious cults. They are hardly works of art. Most are crude and show no sign of being fashioned by specialist craftsmen. The most striking find is of a pair of figures, a male and a female, at Braak (Holstein). Each of them is almost three metres in height. They lay in the peat close to a thick layer of ashes and smashed pottery, the remains of a cult-deposit. A smaller, but still imposing, figure is that of a man from Possendorf (Thüringen), 90 cm. high and shown with one arm raised high above his head. Near him stood a bronze pot and seven pottery vessels, and a little further off lay the skeleton of a man, presumably the victim of a sacrifice.

Occasionally, these stark wooden effigies were placed on a pile of stones thrown up in the centre of a marsh. On such a platform stood the famous male figure of Broddenbjerg (Jutland), a proudly phallic god carved from a single piece of timber. Some of these idols may have been decked out with drapery and ornament which has since perished. A female

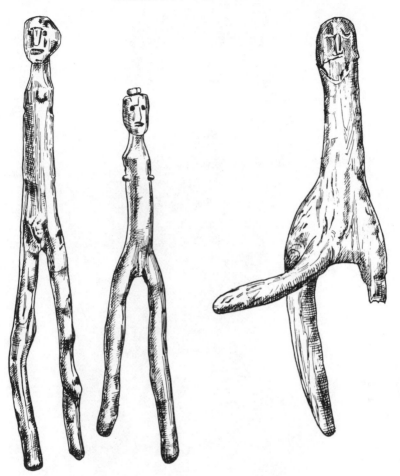

60 *Wooden figures from Braak*
*(Holstein, Germany)*

61 *Wooden fertility figure from*
*Broddenbjerg (Jutland)*

figure from Raebild (Jutland), her breasts and sex organs clearly accentuated, was found close to part of a textile garment which may once have clothed her.

Idols of timber were still being honoured in pagan Germany long after the Migration period. The most famous of all was a huge wooden post or pillar, known as the Irminsul, worshipped by the Saxons. This survived until 772, when Charlemagne cut

*62 Wooden figure from Rude Eskilstrup*
*(Zealand, Denmark)*

it down and then spent three days in destroying the associated sanctuary and looting its gold and silver treasures. Precisely what the Irminsul was is unexplained, for there is no certain evidence for a hero or god called Irmin or anything like it. Was it a fertility figure like those from Braak on an immensely greater scale? Or perhaps it was not a figure at all, but a plain post? The only ancient source to say anything about it states 'that it was a wooden shaft of no mean size, set up in the open air. In their own (Saxon) tongue, they called it Irminsul, which in a Latin translation indicates a pillar of the world, as it were holding everything aloft.' This suggests that the Irminsul was akin to, if not actually identical with, the world-tree of Scandinavian myth.

## SANCTUARIES AND CULT-PLACES

'They do not think it accords with the majesty of divine beings to confine their gods within walls. . . . Their sacred places are woods and groves. . . .' Thus Tacitus, and the other writers say the same thing. Actual buildings dating from the Roman period have not been found, but certain places, for instance those where the wooden figures were erected, clearly had religious significance. Some of the large deposits of war-equipment in bogs may have involved in their ceremonies warriors from a wide area. At two bog-deposits, those of Thorsbjerg and Vimose, a small space was marked off by a wattle fence, and within this enclosure the main deposits were laid in the peat. A rather earlier votive deposit had been made in a spring at Brønderslev (Jutland), a practice frequently encountered among the Celtic peoples. About the spring, thousands of pottery sherds were scattered between several roughly fashioned stone altars. Under the altars, ritual pits contained pottery vessels and other objects. One of the very rare specimens of early German stone sculpture, a crudely carved human head, also stood near the water's edge.

A strikingly unusual site, probably a sanctuary, has recently been excavated at Damp (Schleswig-Holstein). This consists of a number of rectangular enclosures, marked out by rows of stones, and one circle of rather larger boulders, similar to the stone circles familiar in Neolithic and Bronze Age Europe. None of the rectangular stone-settings can be the foundations of houses, or buildings of any kind, and an interpretation as cult-places appears reasonable. They probably date from the late Roman or the Migration period.

From the Migration period, no certain examples of temple-buildings have been identified on the ground, but they must have existed, as literary sources make clear. The great sanctuary of the Svea at Old Uppsala, a beleagured outpost of paganism in eleventh century Sweden, although in use until well after the end of our period, gives the fullest available picture of a pagan temple. Adam of Bremen, writing in the late eleventh century, described it thus: 'A golden chain surrounds the temple, hanging round the steep roof, shining from a distance on those approaching, all the more because the sanctuary itself, placed in an open field, is surrounded by mounds so placed as to form an amphitheatre.' Beneath the mediaeval church of Gamla Uppsala, a timber structure has been examined and identified as the heathen sanctuary described by Adam, but the Swedish excavator's interpretation has not been accepted by all. If he was correct, the ground-plan of the temple revealed by post-holes was almost square, but no details of its superstructure and furnishing survived to be recovered by excavation.

Oak groves continued in use as sanctuaries for long after the period of Migration. They enjoyed an extraordinary survival among the Prussians, some of whom remained heathen until the sixteenth century. As late as that time the god of thunder and others were worshipped among oak-trees. Their images were kept in the trunk of a tree and before that of the thunder-god there burned a fire which was never allowed to go out.

For the most part, the furnishings of the early sanctuaries can only be imagined. But now and again archaeology allows a view of the objects used in them. The most astounding archaeological find which can be associated with a sanctuary is a great hoard of twenty-two gold objects found in 1837 at Pietroassa (or Petrossa) in Rumania. This incomparable cache of fine gold-work comprises cups, tall slender vases with handles, a richly ornamented gold bowl, a huge gold plate weighing seven kilos, two multiangular open-work cups with graceful animals as handles, and several items of ornament, including brooches and a collar. Several pieces, including the great plate, were made in Roman workshops, but the greater part are products of barbarian craftsmen. The whole ensemble must have belonged to some Gothic sanctuary rather than to an individual king, and the likeliest occasion for its secretion in the ground is the Hun attack on the Visigoths in 376.

Another find of sacred objects, a pair of gold horns from Gallehus in Danish Schleswig, has a history as extraordinary as its intrinsic character. The first of the two to be found turned up in 1639, when a lacemaker stubbed her toe on it while walking through the village of Gallehus. The other remained hidden and unsuspected until 1734, when it was dug up by a peasant. Both were placed in the royal collections at Copenhagen and for the next sixty years they stimulated the production of endless books and studies purporting to interpret them. In 1802, they were stolen and melted down. Fortunately, engravings made in the eighteenth century recorded their decoration fully and accurate copies have been produced. Both horns were of solid gold, one somewhat larger than the other.

*63, 64 Gold eagle brooch and multiangular cup from the Pietroassa (Rumania) treasure*

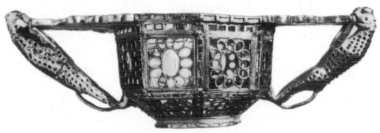

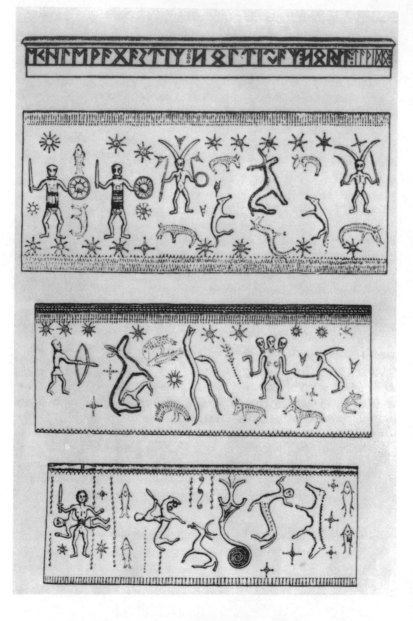

65  One of the golden horns from Gallehus (Schleswig), now lost

The larger bore a runic inscription which records its maker: 'I, Hlewagast, son of Holt made the horn.'

Both bear many figures of men and beasts cut from gold leaf and soldered on, and the field between these figures is adorned with punched designs of more animals, and fish, together with spirals, stars and other patterns. These minor elements in the design point to an origin in the north and not in the Celtic lands or in the Black Sea regions. The human and animal figures have been the main subject of debate, as they probably will always be. As will be seen from the drawing, they include a three-headed figure holding an axe in one hand and leading a goat with the other, another man holding a sickle and drawing along a horse, two horned figures, of whom one is holding a sickle, various kinds of quadruped and snakes, and a centaur. Some figures are found on both horns and the two are plainly linked in their symbolism and its presentation.

While it is impossible to interpret this entire menagerie of myth and cult-ceremonies, there are strong suggestions in several scenes of seasonal observances. The figures occupied in dancing and acrobatics could represent rites concerned with bringing back the sun after the winter. The scene showing an archer shooting at a deer and a snake suckling their young might represent a conflict between fertility and darker powers. The three-headed figure and his goat calls up echoes of the appearance of similar creatures at weddings and winter festivals in medieval and later Europe.

Attempts have been made to identify many of the northern gods in the figures: Thor in the three-headed creature, Tiwaz or Freyr in the dancing men. Few of these, if any, have a convincing basis. It seems safer to attempt to identify the scenes as cult and ceremony, rather than divine actions and myth. The two horns must originally have hung in some sanctuary in Schleswig, though apparently not at Gallehus itself. They probably made their way there as loot. Some of the minor details of the ornament enables them to be dated to the early fifth century.

The organisation of the priesthood has already been touched on in Chapter 2. It remains to outline the part played in religious affairs by women. Their special *forte* was the field of divination and witchcraft. Some seeresses were so honoured by the Germans of Tacitus' time that they were raised almost to the level of goddesses. At least two wielded considerable political influence. A certain Veleda—the name means seeress—played a leading part in the revolt of the Batavi and other Germans against Rome in AD 69. Her prophecies were made from a tower in which she had installed herself, away from the eyes of men, and they were conveyed to the outside world by one of her relatives. The rebel leader Civilis clearly relied heavily on her support, and some embassies were received by Civilis and Veleda's representative in joint session. Her influence must have been felt far outside the borders of her own tribe, the Bructeri.

The Germans were much given to divination and in the *Germania* we hear of three methods of taking auspices. In one, a branch of a fruit-tree was broken up into pieces, the pieces given marks or symbols and then thrown into a white cloth. Then the officiant, a priest in a public ceremony and the father on a family occasion, looked towards heaven, picked up three of the sticks one by one and interpreted the import of the symbols on them. Another means of finding out what the future held in store was to observe the flight or the songs of birds. This practice is recorded in many other parts of the world, including Roman Italy. The most interesting, and we are told the most trusted, of German methods of divination was that which concerned certain sacred white horses kept in hallowed groves. When guidance for a certain course of action was needed, these horses were yoked to a holy chariot by the chief-priest or king, who thereupon walked beside them noting their snorts and neighs. Unfortunately, Tacitus could not, or did not, report how these actually were interpreted. The final kind of divination also has echoes among other primitive peoples. In time of war a captive seized from the enemy of the moment was pitted in single combat against their own champion and the way the duel went indicated the eventual outcome of the war.

The marks or symbols scratched on pieces of wood inevitably recall the odd runic alphabet of the Germanic peoples and although the marks which Tacitus mentions need not have been runes, they were plainly the precursors of them, for runes too were frequently used for the mysterious arts of casting lots and divination. The runic 'alphabet' or *futhark* is a series of

| ᚠ | ᚢ | ᚦ | ᚨ | ᚱ | ᚲ | ᚷ | ᚹ |
|---|---|---|---|---|---|---|---|
| f | u | th | a | r | k | g | w |

| ᚺ | ᚾ | ᛁ | ᛃ | ᛇ | ᛈ | ᛉ | ᛊ |
|---|---|---|---|---|---|---|---|
| h | n | i | j | y | p | z | s |

| ᛏ | ᛒ | ᛖ | ᛗ | ᛚ | ᛜ | ᛞ | ᛟ |
|---|---|---|---|---|---|---|---|
| t | b | e | m | l | ng | d | o |

*66 The early runic futhark*

symbols representing various sounds. Its origin is a much discussed and still baffling question, but the likeliest interpretations derive it from either the Latin or the North Italic scripts. The case for the latter origin is fairly strong. There are notable resemblances between North Italic letters and the runes, and since the script survived in use until about the time of Christ, the Germans could have encountered it in the second or first centuries BC, perhaps in the Alpine regions. An interesting link in the chain of evidence between Italy and the Germans is a bronze helmet from Negau in Austria. This is of a north Italian form and must have been carried by an auxiliary soldier in the Roman forces. It bears a Germanic inscription in North Italic letters, which reads:

harixasti teiva (to the god Herigast) or possibly
harigastiz teivavulfila (Harigast son of Teiwawulf).

The evolution of the runic script is probably directly connected with divination and with magic. This is made clear by many of the names given to individual runes and by the use to which many runic inscriptions have been put. All the runes in the early version of the Germanic *futhark* had a name, and the character of most of the 24 common rune-names obviously points to a connection with cult and with the supernatural. Thus, the rune ᛒ —*terkana,* meaning 'birch-twig', is connected with fertility, the birch in its springtime awakening symbolising the renewal of life. ᚢ —*uruz,* 'aurochs' probably connotes 'manly strength', recalling the power of the hunter which can slay the mighty wild ox. It is known that the auroch was a special target of young German hunters and to kill one and bring his horns to a public assembly was an honoured feat. A few runes actually took their names from gods, for instance ᛏ *tivaz* (the god Tiwaz) and ◇ *inguz* (Ing).

The uses of the runes are clear. A few inscriptions record the maker of the object on which they occur, for instance the famous gold horns from Gallehus. But the great majority are magic or ritual formulae and invocations, designed to perform such things as calming the waves, healing the sick, protecting a man in battle or making a sword invincible. How the script reached the north of Europe is unlikely ever to be known. The earliest instances yet known date from about the late second century AD, so that an origin in the early Roman period is probable. Most would agree with a date of about AD 100. The script never really lent itself to use in literary composition, and most of the early runic inscriptions are short phrases or sentences. Runes, nonetheless, had a long history after the migration period, particularly in Scandinavia and in Anglo-Saxon England. Even as late as the sixteenth century a Swedish admiral could resort to using runes in compiling his diary.

CONVERSION TO CHRISTIANITY

In the fourth and fifth centuries many of the German peoples came into contact with a Christian Roman Empire. Roman Christian churches existed in the frontier lands of Rhine and Danube and Christian bishops played an active role in local affairs, including in some cases the organisation of resistance to the invaders. What dealings had the Christian church with the barbarian tribes? Were attempts made to convert any of them and, if so, how successful were they?

Despite the preparedness of some Germans to be converted, it is a striking fact that there was virtually no *organised* work of

conversion among the peoples beyond the Roman frontiers.
No Roman ruler seems to have drawn the conclusion that the
conversion of large numbers of barbarians to Christianity could
be of use in the political sphere, by neutralising them as foes.
This possibility was at least glimpsed by St. Paulinus of Nola,
who hoped that the conversion of some of the Goths by Bishop
Niceta would mean that they would henceforward live in peace
with the Romans, alongside whom they were now living in the
provinces. There were, then, men like Niceta who laboured to
bring the gospel to the peoples who were crossing or threatening
to cross the frontiers. But their efforts were directed by no
central authority in the Church and their successes were mainly
local successes.

Yet there were conversions among the Germans, even outside the Empire. They came to Christianity by way of Christian
prisoners seized during raids on the Roman provinces and
through the agency of fellow Germans who had served in the
Roman army, been converted during that time and then
returned home to their native land. Possibly Christian traders
active among the Germans also made converts but these men
can rarely have achieved much for the Church. Now and
again, however, they did score a success. A Christian traveller,
probably a merchant, among the Marcomanni in the late
fourth century talked with queen Fritigil of that people about
the great Bishop Ambrose of Milan. Fritigil was so taken with
the account of the redoubtable bishop that she decided to
accept the faith of Christ and wrote to Ambrose himself for
instruction. The bishop took the opportunity to guide the barbarian queen with a letter cast in the form of a catechism. But
even Ambrose would not have sought to make converts among
the Marcomanni if the traveller had not had his talk with
Fritigil.

Apart from these local conversions by prisoners, travellers
and returning Germans, missionary activity beyond the frontiers hardly existed. Conversion of entire peoples to the faith,
with few exceptions, were possible only when the barbarians
settled in the Empire. Thus although Christian communities
existed among the Ostrogoths in south Russia in the fourth
century, that people remained largely pagan until it passed
within the frontiers in the fifth century. Likewise, the Franks,

Alamanni and Burgundians. The Hun empire in central and eastern Europe was a great stumbling-block to Christian missions and the peoples under their sway, who included the Gepids and some of the Rugi as well as the Ostrogoths, could not have undergone conversion until the collapse of the nomad dominion in the middle of the fifth century.

Several major peoples were not converted until much later. The Lombards, according to their own traditions, accepted Christianity towards the end of the fifth century, the Heruls still later. The tribes who were to make up the Bavarians remained outside the faith for long afterwards. Outside the range of missionary activity until a late date, the peoples of the north clung to their paganism for longer still, Frisians and Saxons until the ninth century, the Swedes until later. Even then, large areas of the north defied the Church and its missionaries.

We know most about the progress of Christianity among the Visigoths, the best known of the peoples who migrated to Roman lands. This is principally due to a remarkable Romano-Gothic Christian, Ulfila, who was one of the few fourth century churchmen to work among the barbarians. He was born about AD 311 among the Goths, the child of a Goth and a Roman prisoner captured in Asia Minor. By the time he was 30, he had become a 'reader' in the Gothic Church, the members of which will have been mainly captured Roman provincials. But Goths also took part and the services of this Church were in the Gothic language. At some time before 337, he came as an ambassador of the Goths into the Roman Empire and was consecrated bishop, to serve the Christian communities in the lands of the Goths. He spent seven years in this work, until a Gothic chieftain began a persecution of Christians, causing Ulfila and many others to flee. The remaining 33 years of his life were spent in the Empire, the most important fruit of this long period of labour being a translation of the Bible into Gothic. But Ulfila was a brilliant exception and not many barbarians are likely to have played so important a role in spreading the Christian Gospel.

## FURTHER READING

J. de Vries, *Altgermanische Religionsgeschichte* (2nd edition, De Gruyter)

E. O. G. Turville Petre, *Myth and Religion of the North* (Weidenfeld & Nicolson)

H. R. Ellis Davidson, *Gods and Myths of Northern Europe* (Pelican); *Pagan Scandinavia* (Thames & Hudson)

R. W. V. Elliott, *Runes: An Introduction* (Manchester Univ. Press)

P. V. Glob, *The Bog People* (Faber & Faber)

# 7

# Death and burial

In dealing with an immense geographical area over a span of 500 years, a great deal of regional and chronological variation in burial practices and grave-ritual is to be expected. Thus, in some areas, notably in Scandinavia, barrows or burial mounds were commonly thrown up over the dead whereas in many regions of continental Germania they are unknown or tightly localised. Again, the practice of burying weapons with dead warriors was far from universal: indeed in several areas, probably for religious reasons, it was wholly unknown. Only the more striking and significant features of early German funerals and graves can be picked out, and these are in the main the aspects which archaeological evidence can be specific about. On many aspects of burial, however, archaeology is wholly silent and thus there are many things that we will never know.

THE FUNERAL BANQUET

When the Germanic peoples first entered upon the wider stage of early European history in the first century BC, the prevalent burial rite was cremation. Inhumation graves occur in a few rather limited areas, but these are occasional. The ashes of the dead were usually carefully separated from the débris of the funeral pyre, perhaps in continuance of an age-old practice of loosing the spirit from its earthly bonds, but this custom was shortly to die out. The cremated remains were then placed in a pottery urn, or sometimes a bronze vessel, which was then buried in an unmarked pit or placed beneath a cairn of stones or low mound of earth. In Scandinavia these cairns and burial mounds continued to mark graves, both cremations and in-

*67 The Mandhøj (Bornholm) mortuary house*

humations, down to Viking times and beyond. Occasionally a
death- or mortuary-house was erected over the cremated body.
At Mandhøj on the Danish island of Bornholm a tent-like
structure of branches was erected over the ashes after these had
been covered with earth. When the mortuary-house had stood
for a time it too was set on fire and allowed to collapse over the
grave. The site of these ceremonies was then covered over with
a mound of earth and stones.

The goods provided to accompany the dead into the grave
were mainly objects of personal ornament, tools and weapons.
The weapons, particularly the swords, were often broken or
bent, no doubt as a symbolic act, though its meaning is not
certain. Possibly these slighted weapons signified the breaking
of the owner's power. But the most consistent feature of the
cemeteries of the Roman Iron Age is the presence in the graves
of all the necessary requirements for a feast. Both inhumations
and cremations were accompanied by sets of pottery vessels,
including large containers for holding drink, handled bowls

and cups for drinking from, platters for solid food, and such things as knives and spoons to assist in its consumption. Joints of pork and lamb, and drink of various kinds were laid in the grave too.

This was a new development of the final two centuries BC, and shortly afterwards there came another striking change in burial rites. Suddenly, the richest members of society in northern Germania began to inhume their dead, probably as a result of contact with the Celts. Some of these graves were in the form of wooden chambers, others in Jutland massive stone chambers harking back to much earlier megalithic tombs. The link between these various kinds of tomb was the funeral feast, celebrated at the interment of men, women and children alike.

What form did this ritual take? Was it purely symbolic, or did the relatives of the dead person actually partake of a meal at the side of the grave? Or was it the ancestors of the dead who were the providers of the banquet, in welcome for the incoming spirit? It is impossible for us now to decide between these. What is beyond all question is the strength of the belief which lay behind the ritual. Funeral feasts continued to be celebrated in parts of northern Europe until quite recently, food and utensils being placed in the grave following the ancient custom. We might note in passing that in these feasts the dead were believed to take part. One idea which lay at the bottom of the banquet for the dead may have been actual assistance for the spirit in the other world rather than simply a rite of memorial. The spirit may have required sustenance and support in its first vulnerable period beyond death: the notion of the spirit's wandering before achieving peace is explicit in later sagas. The banquet equipped it for the journey into the uncertain and unseen. The mortuary-houses like the one at Mandhøj may reflect the same belief in the vulnerability of the spirit immediately after its entry into its new sphere of existence.

CREMATION AND INHUMATION

For many centuries before the first encounter between the Germans and literate peoples, the usual rite of burial in Germania had been cremation. We must go back to the Bronze Age to find any notable concentration of inhumation graves, and when we do come across them they are the richly furnished burials of northern chiefs. Throughout the pre-Roman Iron Age, cremation held sway and by about 100 BC, if not earlier, burial of the ashes in an urn placed in a shallow pit had become widespread in the north. This practice was to continue until the Migration period, most conspicuously in the basins of the Elbe and the Weser. Here, enormous cemeteries are known, dating from the fourth and fifth centuries, some of them containing 2,000 urn-burials or more. Against this background of ubiquitous cremation, the recorded inhumation graves stand out sharply. There are two concentrations of them, both consisting of richly furnished burials.

The first is a group of burials distributed between the Vistula and the Elbe and stretching from central Germany to Jutland. They are usually known as the Lübsow group, after the site near Stettin in Pomerania where no less than five have been discovered. The best known examples, however, occur in Scandinavia. The graves were occasionally covered by an earth mound, but more commonly were simply pits in which the dead lay in wooden coffins. The grave-furniture was rich—in some cases outstandingly so, including Roman drinking-sets, glassware, bronze vessels, toilet articles such as mirrors and combs, and locally produced ornaments, especially rings, hair-pins and belt-fittings.

One member of the Lübsow group is the grave from Hoby (Laaland), with its superb silver table-service (p.15): another is a remarkable double burial from Dollerup in south Jutland. Here, the bodies, one of a man, the other of uncertain sex, had lain in coffins made from hollowed out sections of oak trees. Each had an under-blanket, or possibly a shroud, of cow-hide. Both were well supplied with pottery vessels and personal adornments, mainly of native character, and one corpse had by its side two silver drinking cups on a wooden tray. Like the other graves of this group, the Hoby and Dollerup interments did not include weapons: spurs were the only equipment of the warrior to accompany these men to their tomb. But we cannot assume from this that these chieftains were pacific *nouveaux riches* who had settled down to co-existence with the Roman Empire, whose borders now lay not far away to the south and west. Nothing can have been less likely. These men went into their graves unarmed for reasons connected with their peculiar

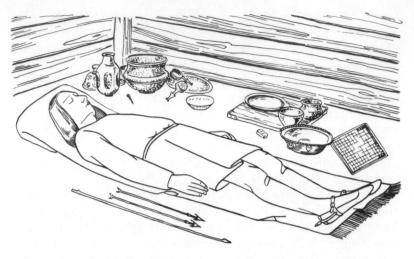

*68 Chieftain's grave from Leuna (near Merseburg, Germany)*

burial-rites and not because their way of life knew nothing of war.

The chieftains' graves of the Lübsow type date in the main from the first century AD. Three centuries later they are paralleled by a rather similar series of rich inhumations, found in the basin of the River Saale in the centre of Germany. These are mostly graves of men, buried in wooden coffins or wood-lined grave-pits. Like the earlier chieftains, these men took imported Roman bronze ware and pottery with them. But they had weapons too: silver arrow heads, spears and javelins as well as spurs, brooches and personal ornaments.

In a few cases, there are signs of rituals conducted at the grave-side. At Leuna, a grave in the Saale group lay close to a pit, which contained the skull and lower leg bones of a horse. These must be the remnants of a horse sacrifice of a kind which spread westward from the nomadic peoples of the Russian steppes. Among some of those peoples, horse sacrifices con-tinued to be celebrated until quite recently. In those ceremonies the greater part of the animal was eaten after its slaughter, and the skin was then hung up on a pole until it rotted away. The heads and hoofs were buried in the ground. An aura of sanctity seems to have surrounded animal skins in many parts of ancient Europe, including the Celtic lands, as may be deduced from their use in divination. Possibly the Leuna grave had been the scene of a ceremony involving a skin and this may have been buried along with the other parts of the horse.

Once again we can observe the close association in men's minds between fertility, here symbolised by the horse, and the after-life. The horse-sacrifices, however, were not only celebrated in cemeteries. Several have been evidenced in peat-bog deposits, and another within a settlement, at Sorte Muld on the island of Bornholm. In one area, among the Saxons in Westfalen, the burials of entire horses are frequently found among the graves of men and women. These appear not to be associated with individual warriors and probably represent a ritual.

The great urnfields of cremation burials in northern Germany, the most celebrated of which are those in the Saxon regions about the lower Elbe (for instance, Westerwanna and Perlberg bei Stade) were in continuous use over several centuries. Westerwanna itself extends from the first century AD to the sixth, although the greatest number of graves date from the third and fourth centuries. Many of these urnfields have been shown to consist exclusively of either male or female burials. Unfortunately, too many of them were carelessly excavated long ago for us to conclude that this was normal practice in the north, but the custom of segregated cemeteries is attested from the Weser to the Vistula. The grave-goods commonly consisted of only one urn in which the ashes were contained. When other objects do occur, they are usually rather humble personal ornaments and toilet articles: combs, shears, brooches, beads, bracelets and rings. Very occasionally objects which might have borne a ritual significance, such as whetstones, are also recovered from such graves. Weapons and other items of wargear are found rather rarely.

Further north, in Jutland, the prevailing burial customs were very different. Here, large urnfields are quite unknown. By contrast, the cemeteries are rather small and they consist of inhumations as well as cremations. The most striking of the Jutland inhumation graves are those in the north of the peninsula. They often have a lining of large stones and occasionally in addition a timber chamber in the centre. Normally a lavish array of pottery vessels was laid out with the dead

person, though now and again the mourning relatives econo-
mised by placing sherds of pottery in the grave as substitutes
for entire pots. The male burials occasionally had weapons in
them. The cremations from north Jutland are much less richly
furnished, containing only pins and other dress ornaments.
This sharp distinction between the two rites of burial is height-
ened by the fact that the two forms do not occur in the same
cemetery.

In central Jutland and in Lower Saxony 'mixed' inhumation
and cremation cemeteries do occur, particularly in the late
Roman period. Probably the practice of inhumation reached
these areas from the north of the Jutland peninsula, although
some scholars have suggested a northward spread from the
Roman provinces, the agents being Germans returning to their
homes after service with the Romans.

Another region where both cremation and inhumation were
practised was Norway, southern Sweden and the Baltic
islands of Bornholm and Gotland. Here the erection of mounds
or cairns of stones over graves continued throughout the Iron
Age down to the Migration period—long after it had been
abandoned or pushed into the background in other parts of
northern Europe. Several of these mounds cover imposing
burials, but the great majority are clearly no more than the
graves of the peasantry. A good example of a richly furnished
barrow is that from Saetrang (Ringerrike, Norway), dating
from the late fourth century. This was a double grave, the dead
and their grave-offerings being placed within a wooden
chamber and the whole covered by a stone cairn. The bodies
were those of a man and a woman, richly clad and lying on
bear-skins. Their grave-goods included weapons, drinking
vessels, buckets, pottery, jewellery and gaming pieces. The
most unexpected feature of the Saetrang burial, however, was
the shape of the cairn itself. Normally these are roughly circular
or oval. This one was shaped like a four-pointed star with
curving points, resembling a swastika or a whirling wheel. Both
these symbols occur on other objects of the Migration period,
in several cases being associated with burials or memorial
stones.

As with several of the Elbe-Weser urnfields, numerous Scandinavian cemeteries were in continuous use for centuries. The

barrow cemetery at Vallhagar (p. 56) is one instance. An even more striking example is the great cemetery at St. Kannikegård on Bornholm. Here the burials range from well before the birth of Christ down to the Migration period.

The burial customs of the north Germans were subject to no sweeping changes during the late Roman and Migration periods. We have seen that in Scandinavia the burial rites of the fifth and sixth centuries were broadly similar to those of the Roman Iron Age. In the Saxon coastlands about the Elbe estuary the urnfields remained the normal cemetery form. It was quite a different story with the Germans who moved southward to seek their fortunes in the Roman provinces. The burial rites of the Franks and Alamanni in the third century are virtually unknown, but it may be presumed that like their forebears in west and central Germany they normally cremated their dead. The earliest cemeteries that we can confidently identify as Frankish and Alamannic, however, are cemeteries of inhumations, in which the graves are arranged in clearly defined rows, the heads of the bodies being aligned to the west. These cemeteries (*Reihengräber*, as they are generally known) are found in Roman frontier areas from the Low Countries to the Danube. From them we have learned almost all we know of early Frankish and Alamannic art and culture.

The earliest Frankish graves which we can distinguish clearly occur in northern Gaul and the Rhineland. Here in certain late Roman cemeteries of the period from about the middle of the fourth century to the early fifth, there are a number of graves which stand out from the remainder not only by their richness but also by the kind of objects they contain. These objects were foreign to those of the Gallo-Roman population but are familiar in a Germanic context. In the graves of men we find weapons, spears, throwing-axes and occasionally swords. In those of women, dress ornaments are common and many of these are of Germanic types. Since many of the graves can be dated by means of the Roman pottery and glassware in them to the late fourth and early fifth centuries, i.e. to a time when Roman authority was still a real force, the Germans buried in graves of this kind must have entered the Empire with Roman sanction. We know from contemporary authors that barbarians were freely employed in this region, many of them as regular soldiers and some as officers of high rank. These are their graves.

Out of many fine examples we may examine one closely. In 1885 during the excavation of a late Roman cemetery at Vermand in northern France, a stone coffin was found, surrounded by a ditch and covered by a mound. Despite some plundering of the contents of the coffin, almost certainly by one of the workmen employed by the French excavators, the grave proved to be furnished in splendid style. Inside the sarcophagus lay a sword, the remains of a belt and an oval plate of silver. Outside it were found the remains of a superb shield, originally decorated with purple leather and sheets of gold foil. Its boss had been covered by a silver-gilt sheet. A group of weapons included a *francisca,* ten spear-heads, and a larger spear-head inlaid with silver. Close by lay the grave of a woman, probably the officer's wife. She had been laid to rest wearing a necklace of large gold beads, three pairs of brooches, a gold ring, and two silver-gilt disc-brooches. Obviously this warrior and his confreres known from other cemeteries held a position of high authority in the regions of northern Gaul.

There are many other barbarian graves of humbler rank. One of the most interesting cemeteries is that at Furfooz in Belgium. The German dead were here laid in a disused Roman bath-house: the sites of ruined buildings were often used as burial places at this time. None of the graves were outstandingly well furnished. A typical grave contained a glass vessel, usually a drinking cup, a few pottery vessels, all of Roman manufacture, a bone comb, the mounts and buckle from a military belt, one or more spears and a throwing-axe.

SHIP-BURIAL

The most familiar burial rite of the northern Germanic peoples is that in which the dead were laid to rest in a ship or in a monument which was shaped like one. Grave-monuments consisting of groups of stones arranged in the form of a ship and the actual interment of boats and ships containing the remains of the dead and their grave-goods have a very long history in the north, above all in Scandinavia. Stone monuments in ship-form were being erected from the Bronze Age onward, although the greater number date from the Migration and

Viking periods. Few seem to have been put up during the Roman Iron Age. The ship we have already met in religious symbolism (p. 130), being carried or drawn in processions connected with rites of fertility. It played an important role in funerary ritual too, probably symbolising the journey of the dead beneath the earth.

The stone settings in the form of ships are particularly common in southern Sweden and the island of Gotland, with a few outliers in Denmark and Norway. Boat- and ship-graves of the Migration period also occur in numbers in Denmark and southern Sweden (and in the British Isles), but they are commonest around the coasts of Norway. These burials were not simply designed for warrior-chiefs. Women as well as men were laid to rest in this way, both in the Bronze Age and in the post-Roman centuries.

Ship-burial took several forms. The dead man could be placed on board a vessel which was launched out to sea, in some cases having been set on fire. The most moving account of a funeral of this kind is that telling of the passing of king Scyld in *Beowulf*.

> Then, at the fated hour, Scyld, a man most valorous, departed to go into the keeping of the Lord; his beloved friends carried him to the sea's flood, as he himself had asked when he, protector of the Scyldings, still ruled them with his words. Dear prince of his country, for long he reigned. There, at the landing-place, the ring-prowed vessel lay, the prince's ship, covered with ice and eager to start. They laid then the beloved chieftain, giver of rings, on the ship's bosom, glorious by the mast. There were brought many treasures, ornaments from far-off lands. Never have I heard that a vessel was more fairly fitted out with war-weapons and battle-raiment, swords and coats of mail. On his bosom lay a host of treasures, which were to travel far with him into the power of the flood. They furnished him with no lesser gifts and royal treasures than those had done, who, in the beginning, sent him forth over the sea alone, child as he was. They set besides a golden standard high above his head, and let the sea bear him—gave him to the ocean. Their soul was sad, their spirit sorrowful. Counsellors in hall, mighty men beneath the heavens cannot say truly who received that load.

In another form of the rite, the ship and its dead passenger and his possessions were burnt on the land and the remains then incorporated in a mound or grave-pit. Archaeology has most to say about a third form of ship-burial, in which the vessel containing the dead, his gear for the journey and sometimes a few of his servants, was laid in the ground unburnt. Though many such burials have been found (the most famous being the cenotaph of an East Anglian king at Sutton Hoo in Suffolk), often they have been plundered centuries before and the finest objects looted. But a good idea of the pomp surrounding these funerals is gained by examining the ship-burials from Vendel and Valsgärde in Sweden, male burials which date from the seventh to twelfth century. Although strictly outside our period, they give the clearest picture of the pattern followed by the rite.

In the earlier graves the dead man was laid in the stern facing the prow, often lying on a couch. Weapons and armour went with him, as well as ornaments. In the fore-part of the ship lay the equipment needed for the voyage, the cooking utensils, buckets, ship's gear, food, and sometimes servants. Animal sacrifices accompanied the burial, the bodies being laid either in the ship or elsewhere in the grave. Horses, a cow or bull, dogs, sheep, pigs, ducks, geese and even a hawk companioned some chieftains into the next world. The ships themselves lay with their bows pointing out to sea, as though ready to sail.

The ship carried the dead to the spirit-world beyond the sea, to the realm governed by Odin. This must be the meaning of the vessels loaded as if for a voyage and of the fact that the great majority of ship-burials occur on or near the coast. But the ship had been for long a symbol of fertility and as such could well represent an appropriate power for the protection of the dead.

ROYAL BURIALS

Kings of the Migration period and their consorts naturally were buried in splendid style, the kings with their war equipment, and their womenfolk with their jewels and fine raiment. Apart from some of the ship-burials which may well be of royal personages, we have knowledge of four tombs which can be called royal, all of them Frankish. The most celebrated, though now largely lost to us, is the grave of Childeric, the father of Clovis (died 482), found at Tournai in 1653. At the time of discovery, the remains could be identified as those of Childeric for they included a gold signet ring bearing his name and portrait. The burial equipment of the king included two richly adorned swords, a spear, an axe and the head of a horse with its harness —yet another horse sacrifice—as well as many pieces of personal adornment and 200 silver and 100 gold coins. On his cloak were sewn 300 cicadas, symbolising immortality. Sadly, this immensely important collection of grave-goods was plundered while on display in Paris in 1831 and now only a few items survive.

Nothing is known of the immediate context of Childeric's tomb: whether it lay on its own or with other burials, or in a structure of some kind. But we are more fortunate in the case of the other royal Frankish tombs, recently excavated beneath the cathedrals of Cologne and St Denis in Paris. The St Denis burial is of a woman of about 45 years, short, slightly built and with fair hair. Her body had been embalmed and laid on a red blanket or cloak within a stone sarcophagus. She had been dressed in fine garments and a dazzling array of jewellery, some of it massive enough to seem more appropriate to a man. Again an inscribed ring allows the body to be identified. This was Arnegundis, a consort of the Merovingian king Chlotar I, and she died about 570. Since she was buried beneath a Christian church, it is no surprise that there is little of pagan ritual in the grave furniture, no magic amulet or funeral banquet.

Two further burials, deep below Cologne Cathedral, one of a woman, the other of a boy of six, were furnished with a wealth of goods appropriate to royalty. Both lay in

69 *The grave of St Arnegunde at St Denis (near Paris)*

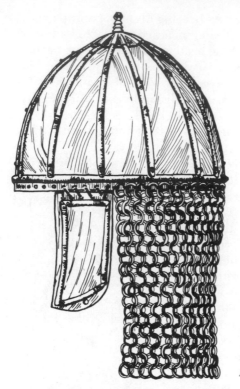

70 *Helmet from boy-prince's grave beneath Cologne Cathedral. The cap is made up of pieces of horn*

stone-lined burial chambers. The woman had probably been laid out in fine clothing and, like Arnegundis, she wore a formidable display of jewels. But unlike the burial at St Denis, some food and drink had also been provided. The boy's grave contained several unique objects, a chair and a little bed, a tiny wooden sceptre, a little helmet with its cap made from plates of horn, as well as a sword, throwing-axe, spear and lance. Both interments date from the middle of the sixth century. Cologne Cathedral lies within the walls of the Roman and early medieval city. Persons buried beneath an intramural church can only have been members of the royal family or the highest ecclesiastical notables. Clearly it is the former that we are here dealing with. These are graves of members of the royal house of the Merovingian Franks.

# 8

# The craftsmen

METALWORKERS

Since the discovery in 1654 of the richly furnished grave of the Frankish king Childeric, who was buried at Tournai (Belgium) in 482, it has been recognised that in ornamental metalwork the achievement of the Migration period craftsmen was not surpassed until the Renaissance. Childeric's grave-goods also testified, later scholars have realised, to the far-reaching contacts of German craftsmen in the fifth and sixth centuries. In the wealthiest graves it is possible to discern styles of ornament and techniques of working which link the Frankish and Alamannic realms with Scandinavia, Italy, the Near East and the Black Sea regions. This was the greatest, indeed the only, barbarian contribution to European art-styles. The foundations for the marvellous achievements of the Migration period craftsmen were laid far back in the Germanic Iron Age, but the really significant advances in decorative techniques were made in the fourth century. It is impossible to tell the whole story in the narrow compass of a few pages. Here we can only take note of the major techniques used in decorative work, principally on jewellery and weapons. Before turning to these, some comment on the general character of early Germanic art is required.

It is somewhat exaggerated to assert that there was no truly Germanic art in the Roman Iron Age. But the exaggeration is pardonable. The decorative arts had a very limited scope before the fourth century. When ornament does appear on metal vessels, brooches and pottery, it rarely, if ever, has any claim to originality. The influence of imported Roman things, particularly metalwork, is everywhere apparent and the finest of all art- and cult-objects found in free Germany were the

products of Celtic and not Germanic craftsmen: the Brå caul-
cron, the Gundestrup bowl and the Dejbjerg carts. Even as late
as the early Migration period, the ornamental styles and metal-
working techniques current among the Germanic peoples were
not of purely Germanic stock, though the northern craftsmen
made them their own.

The Germanic artists were not interested in naturalistic or
representational art. Ornament pure and simple was their
stock-in-trade, and the styles they developed were the result of
their exploration of the great ornamental possibilities presented by animal forms. They discovered how crouching and
curled animal shapes could fill up awkward spaces on brooches
and mounts. The animals they created took over the main
design, becoming serpentine creatures with backward turning
heads, or sea-horses with twisting tails, or nameless monsters
with bird-like heads and beaks. When human beings appear in
this world, which they do rather rarely, their bodies are
elongated or contorted. It was a short step to show combina-
tions of figures: fantastic beasts creeping after a man, a sea-
horse with another monster on its back. It is conceivable that a
few of the grotesque struggles between men and monsters which
are shown represent scenes from myth, but it is tedious and
unnecessary to attempt to identify them.

These magnificent designs are the purest ornamental art,
making a direct and unsophisticated appeal to the eye. The
animal-styles from their beginnings in the fourth century
endured in the north for the next seven centuries and more.
They were by no means confined to metalwork. The Scandinavian picture-stones, which begin in the later fifth century,
felt their influence, and decorated woodwork, all too little of
which has survived, was also treated in this way.

After the animal styles, the most distinctive feature of fine
Germanic metalwork is the use of precious stones, especially
garnets, set in gold. Like the decorative styles this did not
originate in the north. The Goths settled in the Black Sea
hinterland first learnt the technique from their nomadic
neighbours and carried it westward. Some of the nomads themselves, principally the Huns, brought this exciting metalwork to
the west—one of few things on the credit side for this incredibly
savage and destructive people. These contacts between Ger-

mans and nomads brought westerners into touch with art traditions which had grown up far to the east. Now and again this contact with the Orient is made explicit by the objects themselves. On the back of a gold amulet set with small garnets found at Wolfsheim in Rheinhessen there is in Persian script the name of the Sassanid king Ardashir (AD 226–41), who had been dead more than two centuries when the object finally accompanied a Gothic or Hun warrior into his grave.

The techniques employed in the decorated jewellery and weapon ornaments of the north were all of great antiquity: some had already been known in the northern Bronze Age more than a thousand years earlier. How they were drawn into the manufacture of lavish ornaments during the late Roman Iron Age is still unexplained, but German craftsmen became masters of them all. The basic technique for making decorated brooches, buckles and the like was the casting of metal in two-part moulds made of clay. This technique gradually replaced the 'lost-wax' or *cire-perdue* process of casting as the demand grew for identical pairs of brooches. A remarkable degree of fine detail was achieved by using clay moulds alone, although in some cases delicate finishing called for the use of engraving tools. Engraving of ornaments which had received their basic form by casting was a very common decorative technique in the Iron Age and in the fourth century it underwent a major development. Engraving involved the incision of the design by using fine gravers or burins and chisels. It has much in common

71   *Chip-carved buckle from Cuik (Limburg, Holland)*

with wood-working and probably wooden or bone patterns were used as models for designs in metal.

The similarity with wood-carving is clearest in the kind of engraving known as chip-carving *(Kerbschnitt)*, in which rather involved patterns were produced by V-sectioned incisions. The basic shapes of chip-carving were stars, rosettes, squares, triangles, pyramids, zig-zags and meander patterns. Later, leaf and animal ornament began to appear. The chip-carved bronzes, mainly brooches, buckles and mounts for belts, are the commonest of engraved objects, being found not only in free Germany but also in the Roman frontier provinces, where they formed part of the uniforms of the late Roman army. The period during which this art reached the peak of its achievement was the later fourth and early fifth century. Engraving of the precious metals was also practised, the largest class of object being silver utensils and mounts, which were often further embellished by stamping, by niello-work or by gilding.

Closely allied with engraving is chasing. In this technique

*72  Silver  vessel from  Himlinghøje (Zealand,  Denmark)*

*73 Hoard of bracteates and other gold objects from Wiewerd (Holland), seventh century AD*

the pattern is produced in relief by hammering and punching. Chased decoration is found in simple forms from the Roman Iron Age, notably on bronze cauldrons and silver cups imitating Roman models. In the Migration period it became rarer and was not again seriously taken up until Viking craftsmen realised its possibilities. The most interesting of the earlier chased designs are friezes of animals or geometric ornament over which a thin foil of bronze or silver has been pressed.

One of the oldest means of decorating metal is to hammer a punch or die against a prepared surface. Under the influence of Roman models, German craftsmen began to lead stamped ornament into new forms in the late fourth century. Characteristic of their products at this time is the 'star-style', so-called from its common star motif. The Gallehus horns belong here, though their applied figures naturally distract the attention from the lesser ornamental details. Generally, this style appears on stamped silver foils, frequently inlaid with niello. The summit was reached, however, not in the star-style objects, but in

*74    Bracteate
from    Hitzum
(Friesland)*

the bracteates, gold disc-pendants struck in imitation of Roman coins and medallions. The central roundel of the bracteates bears a design modelled on portraits of Roman emperors and struck from the back by an engraved die.

As always, the German artist has liberally adapted his model. The head is greatly enlarged and often is set above a crouching or slinking beast. Around the central panel the larger bracteates have a number of concentric borders covered with fine stamped ornament, often so delicate that the spaces between the stamps can only be picked out by a magnifying glass. These strange ornaments sometimes bear runic inscriptions, a pointer to their association with the supernatural world, and the designs of many of them may represent divinities. Thor, Odin, Tiw and Freyr have been identified by some scholars, plausibly in several cases. But less convincing are attempts to identify the bracteates as representing complex mythological schemes. Obviously they were worn as amulets, giving protection and good fortune to the wearer. This much the runic inscriptions on several of them make clear, with their messages of 'I give luck' or 'Luck for so-and-so'. The divine beings and symbols which were placed on the bracteates, then, probably earned their place as power-symbols and not as conveyors of myth.

The introduction of inlays was an innovation of the Roman Iron Age. The inlays were usually of silver and bronze, but occasionally copper and gilt were used. The inspiration came

from imported Roman metalwork, but north German craftsmen applied the technique to ends which were never envisaged
in the Roman Empire. Some of the products of Scandinavian
craftsmen in particular are indeed minor masterpieces. In its
simplest form inlay is a wire hammered into an engraved
groove in the parent metal. That engraved groove had edges
which inclined towards one another so that the wire was firmly
held in place by the overhang. In later, more elaborate work,
the inlay was made larger than the groove could hold, so that
the surplus metal could be hammered flat in a plate over the
parent surface. Silver and bronze inlay first began to be applied

*75 Bracteate from Åsum (Skåne, Sweden)*

*76 Bracteate from Gerete (Gotland)*

to a wide range of bronze and iron objects in the second century AD.

Among the earliest are the fine buckles from Munkehøjgaard (Laaland) and Smedby (Öland). The Munkehøjgaard buckle is attached to a rectangular plate edged with close-set silver wires and within this frame, the mount is ornamented with silver filigree. The Smedby piece has a plate richly adorned with criss-cross and herringbone inlay in silver, while the buckle itself bears an inlaid pattern of oblique strokes. Beginning at about the same time, inlay was also applied to bronze. The finest examples, however, are the twin spurs from Hörninge, Köping (Öland), with their rich filigree on the flat surfaces and a delicate net of silver inlay covering the pricks. Among items of war-gear, the outstanding piece of a somewhat later period is a sword sheath from Kragehul (Fünen), the bronze mounts of which have both copper and silver inlay. Fourth-century work in this technique merges imperceptibly with that of the Migration period and plainly there was an unbroken continuity in this craft in the region where it reached its peak, southern Scandinavia. It was, however, by no means

*77, 78 Buckles from Smedby (Öland) and Munkehøjgaard (Laaland, Denmark)*

*79 Spur with silver inlay from Hörninge, Köping (Öland)*

confined to the north. Franks, Alamanni, Goths and Anglo-Saxons in Britain all practised work in inlay.

The very pinnacle of gold- and silver-smithing is represented by work in filigree and cloisonné. Filigree work consists of an ornament of wires and tiny globules of metal, most commonly gold. Its near relative granulation uses globules only. The supreme examples of filigree were produced in Scandinavia in the fifth and sixth centuries, although for two or three centuries the technique was being explored. It is hard to pick out 'typical' examples in the varied range of objects we possess, but the gold neck-rings of Ålleberg and Färjestaden, and the scabbard-mounts from Tureholm do at least represent the astonishing quality of the best of this work. Although calling for a dexterous skill, the craft of filigree is essentially simple. Grains of gold or silver were cut from a drawn wire and then placed on a layer of powdered charcoal. When this was heated the metal fragments became spherical. They could then be fastened to wires or to sheets of metal by means of solder or by heating them again and letting them adhere to their new base. The latter method produced the most delicate pieces, the tiny beads of gold seeming to tremble and vibrate at a touch.

During the fourth century, Germanic metalwork was almost

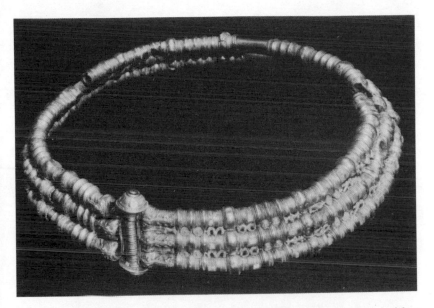

80, 81  Gold collars from Alleberg (Västergötland, Sweden) and Möne
(Västergötland, Sweden)

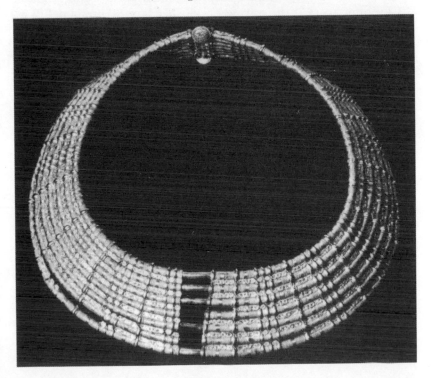

*82 Gold collar from Färjestaden (Öland)*

transformed by the rapid spread of cloisonné decoration from a source among the nomadic peoples of the Black Sea hinterland. Cloisonné work is the setting of polished stones or enamel in a network of small metal cells, themselves often arranged in elaborate patterns. It brought splendour to the goldsmith's art to complement the delicacy of the finest filigree. The most favoured stone for the settings was the garnet, lending a fire-lit glow to jewellery and fine weapons. Garnet cloisonné was employed in almost every part of the Germanic world where gold-working was practised: England, Frisia, Scandinavia, Frankish Gaul and Lombard Italy. The stones were secured in their cells by inclining the metal walls towards each other and to guard against breaking the garnet during the setting, a layer of resin was placed on the bottom of the cell. The brilliance of the stone could be enhanced in various ways: by making the surface slightly convex, or by placing a fragment of gold or silver foil beneath it. In the fifth century and later, the garnets themselves occasionally received an inlay of gold or enamel, and from now on the earlier geometric designs began to give way to flowing animal ornament.

IRON-SMELTING

Much less spectacular but still very informative are the

products and processes of the iron industry. A great deal has been learnt in recent years about the vital craft of iron-smelting, chiefly through excavation of sites where furnaces were active. In the past it has been customary to agree with Tacitus' verdict that the German tribes had relatively little iron at their disposal and the archaeological finds appeared to suggest that iron weapons and other equipment were of poor quality compared with those of the Roman world. This is too one-sided a picture. Analysis of many objects reveals that their quality is comparatively high. Further, the discovery of many smelting hearths and furnaces demonstrates that in most respects German methods of smelting iron were on a par with those of the Roman provincial smiths. The most remarkable furnace sites have been uncovered in Bohemia and Moravia, in Schleswig-Holstein and Denmark, in the Elbe valley, and in southern Poland.

The commonest and simplest kind of smelting installation is the bowl-hearth. This was no more than a hollow, either on the ground surface or deep beneath it, in which the ore was smelted over a fire. The necessary air-flow was provided either by a natural draught or by bellows. But more advanced shaft-furnaces were also known, of a kind which may have originated in the Roman world. These consist of a tall, narrow 'chimney' or shaft of clay, or occasionally of pottery, standing over a hearth. The height of the shaft greatly increased the flow of air over the iron ore in the hearth, so smelting it more effectively.

Unfortunately there is little to be said about the social background of this important industry. We know nothing of the

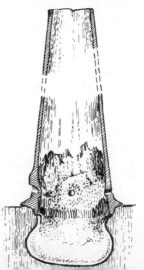

*83 Iron-smelting furnace from Scharmbeck (Harburg, Germany)*

social standing of the smiths although by analogy with other ancient peoples it must have been high. This was not an industry with centralised production centres, even though there were concentrations of furnace-sites near high quality ores. A great deal of iron manufacture must have been in the hands of village craftsmen, making goods to order and, as we saw in the case of the settlement at Feddersen Wierde (p. 45), often in the service of a chief or other leader.

### SHIPBUILDERS

The earliest boats in northern waters of which we have any knowledge are those shown in the many rock-carvings of Norway and Sweden. The great bulk of these fascinating monuments date from the Bronze Age and from the transition to the Iron Age. They frequently show broad, square-hulled vessels, usually with an elevation to fore and aft. The profiles are certainly of craft made of skins, stretched over a timber framework. Such boats would serve for fairly short journeys connected with fishing and seal-hunting, and not dissimilar craft were used until fairly recently near the Arctic Circle. When the Norwegian explorers Nansen and Sverdrup were compelled by circumstances to construct a boat from skins and branches, they produced a serviceable craft which agreed well with the Bronze Age drawings. It is not certain exactly when boats made entirely of timber emerged in the north. Log-boats or dug-out canoes, of course, are found all over Europe from the Neolithic onward, surviving down to the nineteenth century in places. But the log-boat is useless in the sea. For this, plank-built boats were necessary and these may first have appeared during the late Bronze Age.

The earliest more or less complete plank boat which has come down to us is the Iron Age craft from Hjortspring (Als), dating from about 200 BC. This had been sunk in a peat-bog as a votive-offering, together with a great store of weapons and

*84  The Hjortspring ship, about 200 BC*

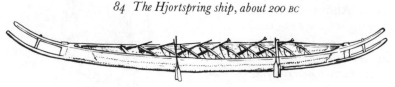

*85 Rock-engraving of a
ship from Brandskogen
(Uppland, Sweden)*

armour. It was, then, an instrument of war. The Hjortspring
boat measures 58 feet in overall length and may have held a
crew of 20 men. It was constructed out of five broad, thin
planks, one at the bottom forming the keel and over it two
planks on either side. The keel-plank and the gunwale extend
beyond the hull to fore and aft, giving the craft a profile well
known from many of the later rock-pictures. The planks, or
strakes, making up the hull have been sewn together with cord
and the holes caulked up with resin. The inner framework was
a ribbing of thin hazel branches lashed on to the strakes.
Greater rigidity was produced by inserting timber cross-struts
at intervals amidships. Not a single iron nail or other metal part
was used to make this ingenious and serviceable boat. As with
the boats of the Bronze Age rock-carvings, there was no trace
of a mast. Propulsion was entirely by means of unfixed paddle
oars, about 20 in all, and steering by a rudder at both bow and
stern.

Compared with the ships of the Viking period, the Hjortspring boat is a primitive vessel, vulnerable to high seas and
swells. But the main aims of its builders were achieved. They
produced a light, seaworthy vessel, able to carry a fairly large
crew. Above all, in the finish of the structure we can detect the
beginnings of that craftsmanship which was ultimately to produce the Viking shipwrights' masterpieces of Tune and
Gokstad.

The ship which has most to tell us about the vessels of the

*86  The Nydam ship, about AD 350–400*

Roman period is the splendid craft from Nydam in Schleswig, which dates from the late fourth century AD. Excavation in Nydam Moss in the 1860s revealed three boats. One was left in the peat, another was destroyed, and the third, the best preserved, was removed for reconstruction and detailed study. Now in Schloss Gottorp Museum in Schleswig, the Nydam ship is one of the glories of northern European archaeology. About 70 feet in length and nine feet wide amidships, this vessel accommodated 15 pairs of oarsmen and a steersman. It was built up from 11 large oak planks, five strakes to each side over a massive keel plank. The gunwales were each made up by two planks jointed together.

As well as being somewhat larger than the Hjortspring boat, the Nydam ship differs in several structural features. First, it possesses rowlocks, 15 to each side, fixed to the gunwales. The oars, then, were to be in fixed positions on the side and not used as paddles as at Hjortspring. Secondly, the overlapping strakes making up the sides were fastened together with iron nails. Fixed rowlocks had already appeared on earlier vessels, for instance on the Halsnøy (Norway) boat of about AD 200. The use of iron nails, however, is new and marks a significant advance. The high quality of the construction is best seen in the attachment of the ribs to the sides. These are not nailed or fastened directly to the inside of the strakes and keel but were lashed with cords to wooden clamps projecting from those timbers. This method of constructing the ribs was a great improvement on earlier means and vastly increased the seaworthiness of the ship. With modifications it was employed later by Viking master shipbuilders. Propulsion was still by means of oars only: there was no provision for a mast. The rudder, 6½ feet long, was found in the excavations but it is not clear how it was attached to the ship. The internal arrangements, too, provoke many problems. There is no trace of any deck. But it is impossible to row on fixed oars without any footrests and the suggestion has been made that the bottom of the boat was filled with stones and these covered by a mat of woven brushwood. Quite apart from providing a convenient flooring, this would act as ballast and increase the stability of the craft. The rowers sat on narrow benches resting on the ribs.

Without question the Nydam vessel was a war-ship, designed to hold as many men as possible. Though probably difficult to manoeuvre compared with later Viking ships, it was a perfectly seaworthy craft. It marks an important stage in the development of shipbuilding, falling rather more than halfway between the skin boats of the Bronze Age and the fine craft of the Vikings. And it can be given a general historical context. It dates from the end of the Roman Iron Age, and ships of this kind may have borne Germanic pirates against the northern coasts of the Roman Empire and carried the first Anglo-Saxon settlers to Britain. Against this, however, is the fact that a rowing boat of this size could travel at a speed of not much more than three knots and thus a journey across the North Sea would have taken several days of continuous rowing. More reasonably then, ships of the kind represented at Nydam were used in the coastal waters of the tideless Baltic. And perhaps ships with sails were known in the north at this time, but have so far not been found.

*87, 88 Rowlock and rudder from the Nydam ship*

OTHER CRAFTSMEN

It is clear enough from the Nydam ship that the art of carpentry was highly developed by the late fourth century. That it was so much earlier is apparent from the remains of houses (p. 65). The making of furniture and wagons must also be presumed, although the evidence for actual manufacture of these in the north is slight. Wooden vessels of high quality were certainly produced. Fine examples of bowls, platters and flasks make it clear that the lathe was known to the early German carpenter. The range of objects produced in wood was very wide, including items of war-gear, buckets, bowls and plates.

The working of bone, horn and antler produced many everyday things: combs, clothing-pins, knife-handles, even certain kinds of tools. A superb range of bone and antler objects has been recovered from the Frisian Terpen. Most of the everyday articles were produced by individual communities, but at some settlements, for instance Feddersen Wierde, specialist workers in bone were active in the service of the local headman.

The skills of weaving were highly developed, as garments of excellent quality from Thorsbjerg and Vehnemoor (Oldenburg) show. Normally clothing was produced by members of individual households. The excavated settlements sometimes include a hut or huts which has plainly served as a weaving shed from the discarded clay loom-weights lying on its floor. Such articles as leather shoes and belts would also be made by individual households, although some leather-working, for instance the manufacture of horse-harness and shield-coverings, was probably in the hands of specialists.

The social status of the craftsmen in free Germany has not been recorded for us. The smiths and jewellers who made fine weapons and ornaments for the leaders probably enjoyed a privileged position in society. This at least is borne out by the existence of smiths' graves, identified by means of the appropriate tools among the grave-goods. These are known throughout the Roman and Migration periods. In the Roman period they are not common, but a significant number has been recorded in Jutland. Whether these men worked in one place, either a settlement-site or the residence of a local chieftain, or whether they travelled from patron to patron is unknown. Possibly both ways of making a living were pursued.

FURTHER READING

W. Holmqvist, *Germanic Art during the First Millenium AD* (Stockholm)

B. Salin, *Die altgermanische Thierornamentik* (Stockholm)

J. Hubert, J. Porcher & W. F. Volbach, *Europe in the Dark Ages* (Thames and Hudson) has fine photographs of metalwork.

A. W. Brøgger & H. Shetelig, *The Viking Ships* (2nd edition) includes a valuable account of early ships in the north from the Neolithic to the Vikings.

# CHRONOLOGICAL TABLE

| BC | History | Archaeology |
|---|---|---|
| c. 350 | Voyage of Pytheas | |
| | | c. 200 Hjortspring deposit |
| c. 115–101 | Invasion of Cimbri and Teutones | |
| 55 & 53 | Julius Caesar crosses the Rhine | |
| 12–AD 16 | Campaigns of Augustus against the Germans | |
| 8–3 | Maroboduus builds his empire | |
| *AD* | | c. 1 Hoby grave |
| 9 | Triumph of Arminius in Teutobergs | |
| 19 | End of Maroboduus' empire | |
| 69–70 | Revolt of Civilis and the Batavians on the lower Rhine | |
| 83–5 | Domitian's campaigns against the Chatti | |
| c. 90–130 | Roman frontier extended from middle Rhine to middle Danube | |
| 98 | Tacitus' *Germania* published | |
| c. 150 | Ptolemy's *Geography* compiled | |
| | | c. 160 Thorsbjerg deposit |
| 166–80 | Wars of Marcus Aurelius against the Marcomanni | |
| c. 180 | Goths migrate from Vistula to south Russia | |
| 213 | Emergence of the Alamanni | |

| AD | History | Archaeology |
|---|---|---|
| 233 | Alamanni ravage Roman provinces of Upper Germany and Raetia | |
| 258 | Emergence of the Franks | |
| 259–60 | Alamanni force evacuation of frontier between Rhine and Danube | |
| c. 275 | Romans abandon Dacia | |
| | | c. 300 Leuna graves |
| c. 350 | Ulfila translates the Bible into Gothic | c. 350–400 Nydam ship |
| c. 375 | Huns break into south Russia and destroy Ostrogothic kingdom | |
| 378 | Visigoths defeat Romans at Adrianople | |
| | | c. 400 Ejsbøl deposit |
| 406 | Vandals and others cross the Rhine and pass through Gaul into Spain | |
| 410 | Visigoths under Alaric take Rome | |
| 429 | Vandals cross from Spain into North Africa | |
| 443 | Burgundians settle in Savoy | |
| 451 | Visigoths defeat the Huns at Troyes | |
| 453 | Death of Attila | |
| 454 | Alamanni occupy Alsace and begin to settle in Switzerland | |
| 476 | Odoacer becomes king in Italy | c. 475 Pietroassa treasure |
| | | 482 Childeric's grave |
| 489 | Theoderic replaces Odoacer as ruler of Italy | |
| | | c. 550 Cologne graves |

# INDEX

Numerals in heavy type refer to the figure-numbers of illustrations